MARCHING ORDERS
A Civil War Diary
by
Alexander Crawford Gwin

Edited by
Joseph Campbell
Judy Gowan

Daisy Publishing
P.O. Box 309
Altoona, Pa. 16603
800-356-7622
Web Site: www.daisypub.com

© 1999 Daisy Publishing
ISBN 0-9670553-1-8

INTRODUCTION

This is the diary of A. Crawford Gwin, a soldier from Altoona, Pennsylvania who fought on the Union side in the American Civil War. He was a member of the Seventy-Six Volunteers, Company F, from Pennsylvania, also known as the Keystone Zouaves. This regiment was mustered in 1861. Company F was from the Blair County area. After being mustered in, the regiment proceeded to Fortress Monroe and then to Hilton Head Island, South Carolina. This is where Company F spent much of their time drilling and policing the fortification and prisoners. Much of the duty was monotonous, and sometimes deadly in the summer heat. However, there were also some very interesting and exciting experiences along the way. As you read this piece of history you will meet many other members of company F and others. Please use the index in the back to locate information on the men you read about. Some of the dates may not coincide because it took a few days for news to reach the mainland. Along with A. Crawford Gwin, the reader will meet his brother James A. Gwin, also known as Alex, and a possible cousin George Gwinn. Many spelling errors were corrected, while some items such as ships, hot air balloons, and medicines were left as Gwin spelled them. He did not use any punctuation when writing and the grammar may seem rough at times. The diary begins on January 1, 1862 and ends February 28, 1863. It is believed by the editor, that Alexander Crawford Gwin completed one diary book and stopped writing, or the second book was lost. Alexander Gwin was killed five months later at the battle of Fort Wagner on July 18, 1863 at the age of 27.

Now take a step back in history with us, and listen to the voice of a young man who would fight and die, as did so many others on both sides of this terrible struggle.

CONTENTS

Introduction

Acknowledgements

Diary of A. Crawford Gwin 1

Conclusion 78

End Notes 80

Company F Roster 82

ACKNOWLEDGEMENTS

Appreciation is given the many people whose efforts and support made this publication possible:

    Susan Heavner-Researcher of the 9th Maine
    Patty Mitchell-Copy Editor
    Sam Kipp
    Capitol Press
    U.S. Army Military History Institute
    Chris Pendleton & Natalie Harvey at the Museum of Hilton Head Island, for sharing their knowledge of Hilton Head during the Civil War years.

Jim Shafer and family for their ambition to have the diary of A. Crawford Gwin preserved and remembered.

Cover, unidentified Zouave soldier of the 76th Pennsylvania Volunteer Infantry.

Matt Marvin's sketch of a Zouave soldier on page 46.

Wednesday, January 1, 1862

Time flies, 1861 has passed quicker apparently than any other previous year of my life. It is now only to be remembered among the past and this day we all want to celebrate the beginning of peace on earth and good will toward men. This year finds me in the midst of a Civil War designed to preserve our noble government and preserve our civil and religious liberty. We have so engaged thousands of the American people as never before on this first day of a new year. The calamity which is up, saw us make this a cause of necessity. Our company was on guard at the breast works watching the cannon being mounted. We camped beside the grand guard. There was a fight at Beaufort today. News reached us that our Regiment and several others had marching orders to be ready in short notice. We were a little chagrinned to think that we would have to stay while our regiment was going off to fight. Fortunately they were not needed and we were relieved at the same time and returned to our quarters safely. We washed some of the dirt off and ate a meager supper and went to bed tired. Rumored today that we had a victory in Beaufort. It was very windy today and this made it very disagreeable. The wind fell towards evening.

Thursday, January 2, 1862

Slept soundly all night. Our Company and Company A were excused from drill this forenoon to clean our guns. They having got dirty from being out all night. Heavy firing was heard in the direction of Beaufort this morning at 10am. The long roll was beaten and fall in quickly was sounded through our quarters. In a short time, the regiment was formed on the parade ground ready to march. We were all eager to get a whirl at the enemy. We were ordered to stack arms and orders not to leave our quarters for the fear we should be called on. The excitement was over in a short time. We had company drill in the afternoon. We went to bed not knowing what the morning would bring. Maybe we would be called out during the night.

January 1st 1862

Time flies 1861 has pased quicker apparently than any other previous year of my life. It is now only to be remembered among the past. And this very day we are want to celebrate as the beginning of "Peace on Earth and good will toward Men" finds us in the midst of a dreadful civil war. We are engaged in it however in a sacred work designed preserve noble government and to preserve our Civil and Religious liberty we have so long enjoyed. Thousands of the American people have this day been employed as they never before have on the first day of a new year. The Calamity which is upon us us makes this a cause of necessity. Our Company was on guard at the work watching the canon that

Friday, January 3, 1862

No alarm was given last night. Slept soundly. The weather was pleasant. We had our usual squad and company drill. Heavy firing was heard in the direction of Beaufort. No reliable news from there.

Saturday, January 4, 1862

Nothing of any importance today. Had company drill as usual.

Sunday, January 5, 1862

Cloudy this morning had dress parade at the usual time at 8:30am. The engineers went to work this morning on the instrument. No work has been done on the Sabbath. Why it is done today, I do not know. It commenced raining very hard just as inspection commenced. With all the rain the ground was not wet more then two inches deep. It is clear this evening.

Monday, January 6, 1862

Clear and warm today. Forty members from our company had fatigue duty[1] today. Had no dress parade. Saw balloon get filled up today. Improvements are being made here in a short time. It begins to appear like home. The Atlantic came in with mail. All were glad to see her.

Tuesday, January 7, 1862

Very pleasant today had squad and company drill as usual. The mail came in today which is always nice.

Saturday, January 11, 1862

Nothing worthy of note has occurred since Wednesday. Warm today. Balloon is being filled today with gas. The captain had our company excused from drill to go to the woods to get bushes to plant in front of our tents. We have the tents carpeted with pine leafs.

Sunday, January 12, 1862

Foggy this morning, then turning warm and pleasant. Slept well last night. The island balloon ascended up a short distance today. Pro Sow will go on a recognizance expedition as soon as the weather will allow. Had preaching today at 10am. Ten men of our company are on fatigue duty today. The men who are on fatigue duty get one jigger per day which I think is wrong for some of are boys to get a little tipsy. It also gives the boys an appetite for spirits which will make habit drunkards in time.

Monday, January 13, 1862

Clear and warm all day. Had squad drill in the forenoon and company drill in the afternoon. Nothing of note happened today. Seen two white ladies today.

Tuesday, January 14, 1862

Clear and warm had company and squad drill as usual.

Wednesday, January 15, 1862

Cloudy and warm had dress parade. Rained some, had no drill today. Island is all sand, raises good corn and cotton.

Thursday, January 16, 1862

Rainy and cold, had no drill of any kind. Windy from the ocean today.

Friday, January 17, 1862

Cool and very foggy till about 10am. Cleared and turned warmer in the afternoon.

Saturday, January 18, 1862

Clear and warm. Had squad and company drill as usual. Stacked tents in afternoon.

Sunday, January 19, 1862

Clear and warm. Had preaching from 1st John 2nd chapter from the 2nd verse.

Monday, January 20, 1862

Had regimental drill after dress and company drill.

Tuesday, January 21, 1862

Had company drill in the a.m.. Company A and Company F were detailed for Provost Guard[2]. The two companies got orders to have everything ready to move in one hour. We ate our dinner struck the tents and started for the area which is in the center of a big swamp. It was very disagreeable place. Dirt was nearly shoe mouth deep. Men were sent to work at once to prepare the quarters. It rained in the evening.

Wednesday, January 22, 1862

Wet and cold all day. I brought in a Rebel prisoner from the wharf. He was captured in North Edesto Island, 7 miles south of Charleston by Captain Amsnen. He was trying to take Negroes off the island and they took him prisoner. Several officers were assigned their duty. My duty is quartermaster[3] for the prisoners. There are 32 prisoners, 15 Rebel and the balance is of Union soldiers.

Thursday, January 23, 1862

Rainy and cold all day. Did not do anything of any account.

Friday, January 24, 1862

Cool and wet, wind blew our tent over last night. Had fun putting it up in the rain.

Saturday, January 25, 1862

Cold and rainy. Brought in another Rebel prisoner. He is a copper colored Negro. Guards took target practice when they came off guard.

Sunday, January 26, 1862

Clear and warm all day. Had dress parade and orders were read to the effect that we would have to drill about 5 hours with other duties. Boys are all down on such orders. Captain Campbell issued them. Our chaplain came down and preached to the prisoners and they were very attentive. Sixteen vessels of the fleet left here today for Fort Pulaski and Savannah

Monday, January 27, 1862

Clear and warm all day. Had dress parade and squad drill. Boys would not turn out to company drill in the pm.

Tuesday, January 28, 1862

Cool and pleasant today. Had dress parade. Private Nathan Brown is best at targets 80 yards from the center. I am second best. Got letter from home and one from Sergeant M. Wrote letter home and to Sergeant M. We can hear cannon firing in the direction of Ft. Pulaski.

Wednesday, January 29, 1862

Cool and pleasant. Had dress parade. Bought $.50 worth of paper and envelopes-cost of all $1.75. Gathered some sea shells today.

Thursday, January 30, 1862

Clear morning. Went to the commissary and got some more paper and took a lesson on sketching from a prisoner. Had squad drill company would not turn out to company drill. Corporal Adie Irwin was the best shot today.

Friday, January 31, 1862

Cloudy. Had dress parade and squad drill. Rained some at 9am. Drawed rations for 26 today. One prisoner brought in a sailor and four discharged. Windy and sand flying everywhere in the evening.

Saturday, February 1, 1862

Clear morning. Draw bread for the prisoners this morning. Took another lesson on sketching today. Gave rations to squad and boat crew. Rained hard in the morning.

Sunday, February 2, 1862

Clear and cool this morning. Corporal Richard Bell and Corporal John Martin went down to the beach to their pickets about 3 miles away. Saw a alligator 9 feet long which was killed by a soldier. There was no preaching in our camp today. This is the first Sunday I have not been in church since we left Pennsylvania.

Monday, February 3, 1862

Clear and cool this morning. Had dress parade and drill as usual. Went to the wharf with Corporal Bell seen a sailor fight. Six sailors were brought to the guard house and released in the evening. Corporal David Moore took sick last night and appears poorly today. Heavy firing was heard in the direction of Savannah. Mail came in today.

Tuesday, February 4, 1862

Cloudy morning. Got letter today. Private James Ayers and I took a prisoner of the 8th Maine regiment to Seabrook about 6 miles away. 32 guns were fired today in the arrival of part of the Burnside Expedition . There were 13 Negroes and one white man brought in by the police today. Corporal Moore is better today.

Wednesday, February 5, 1862

Cool and clear. Went for bread at daylight. Had dress parade and company drill. 4 prisoners came in today. Wrote letter to home. Took a Negro prisoner to the Negro house to stay all night. Seen a white lady today.

Thursday, February 6, 1862

Warm, windy and cloudy. The Negro was discharged today. Alex bought a bushel of potatoes from him. Our regiment moved yesterday from the old camp down to the other old fort called Ft. Wells [4]. Wrote a letter home.

Friday, February 7, 1862

Very warm this forenoon. Cooled off in the afternoon. Had a pretty smart shower of rain. Had no squad or company drill. Had dress parade. Corporal Moore still not well yet. Sergeant Alex Gwin and Private John Kough are not well. Went and got medicine from the doctor. Heavy firing was heard in the direction of Savannah today.

Saturday, February 8, 1862

Clear and warm, clouded up in the forenoon. Had dress parade and company drill. Sergeant James Brown drilled the company. Company drew rations today. Wrote letters home and wrote three letters for Corporal Moore. Alex and John are not well yet but better today. Rained very hard in the evening with heavy thunder. Two prisoners were released today. Never gets muddy here, water sinks into the sand.

Sunday, February 9, 1862

Cloudy morning, rained at 7am. Had no dress parade or inspection on account of rain. Yesterday evening seen carriage with two white gals in it. That made me feel like as if I were at home or in the land of civilization. Took my first sketch of a island in the middle of the swamp yesterday. Teacher said it was very good. Corporal Bell and I took a walk down the beach and came up to the wharf. Seen the Rebel prisoners get on board the steamer Baltic.

Monday, February 10, 1862

Raining this morning and all night. Kough and Smith's tent leaked very much and they got wet. No dress parade. Draw rations for 15 prisoners. Did not rain this afternoon.

Tuesday, February 11, 1862

Warm morning. Had dress parade and company drill. Sketched today. Two prisoners brought in today. The Baltic left here with 11 Rebel Prisoners.

Wednesday, February 12, 1862

Clear morning, got up early this morning. Last night Corporal Bell, Walter Bare and I got passes to travel outside of the pickets. Started at 8am and went to the Drayton Plantation[5] and visited the cotton gin. From there we went up the beach to Eliots Plantation and inspected things. All around a very nice house and yard, all the flowers were destroyed. From there we went to Seabrook. 20 of the Company A and 45th Pennsylvania Vol. camped there. This is where the Rebels crossed over to Pinckney Island and from there to the mainland. This place was taken by the Union troops at the mouth of the Broad River. From here we traveled to Square Pokes Plantation. It is located on the Broad River. one and half miles southeast of Saybrook. This is a very pretty and valuable plantation. From there we went to the Grayhouse Plantation, it is 2 miles south of the last. This is where the major of the 45th has his headquarters. Here we met 6 teams from the fort. Here I seen the prettiest Negro gal I have ever seen. Got into camp late and slept soundly all night.

Thursday, February 13, 1862

Clear morning. Had dress parade and company drill. Wrote letter home and one to Illinois for Corporal Moore. Went to the wharf in the evening D.L. put in the guardhouse for burning.

Friday, February 14, 1862

Clear morning. Went for bread early for prisoners. Went into the woods for firewood in the forenoon. This afternoon fixed our tent, put a floor in it of pine twigs. Got cloudy in the evening.

Saturday, February 15, 1862

Cloudy and rainy a little this morning. Prisoners were very troublesome last night. Some of them were drunk. Had dress parade and company drill as usual. There were 30 beef cattle slaughtered here today. Provo Marshall[6] killed a hog. The first that I seen butchered. One of the prisoners has a ball and chain to his leg for getting drunk and misbehaving. Rained at 4pm and all last night.

Sunday, February 16, 1862

Cloudy and rainy. Had no drill parade or inspection. Stayed in camp all day. Had onions and potatoes for dinner. John Kough cooked them. Rained in the evening at 5pm. Had no roll at night. Went to bed early, slept sound all night.

Monday, February 17, 1862

Very cloudy morning. Went for bread for the prisoners at daylight. Nobody would cook meat for breakfast. So we had to make our own breakfast and coffee. Rained in the evening.

Tuesday, February 18, 1862

Cloudy morning and foggy. Rained in the forenoon. Had no dress parade or company drill. Stayed in tent all day. Cannon firing heard in the direction of Savannah, Ga. Sergeant Joseph Findley returned today after being absent since the 8th.

Wednesday, February 19, 1862

Cloudy this morning and warm. Had no dress parade. Had company drill up at the old camp ground. By Sergeant Joseph Cannon. Was paid at 3pm and received $44.63. Paid Lieutenant Henry Wayne. Sent $30.00 home. Had a great time among the boys.

Thursday, February 20, 1862

Clear morning, had dress parade and company drill. After which Corporal Bell and I went down to the wharf and bought some apples. John Kough bought one pound of butter. We all paid for part of it. Went on guard at 4pm.. Very pleasant night-got cool at 3am..

Friday, February 21, 1862

Cloudy morning and wind blowing from the sea. Had dress parade and short drill by Sergeant Cannon. Large mail came in on the Herrison. She left New York on Sunday the 16th. She is a very old vessel and slow traveler.

Saturday, February 22, 1862

Very foggy this morning. Cleared up at 8am. Had dress parade and company drill. Got mail at 10am. Got letter and paper from C.J.M. of Huntington County. Today at 12:00 a national salute was fired in honor of the birth of Washington and the victory gained by General Burnside's expedition at Roanoke, NC. The salute was fired by the gun boats and heavy guns on the fort and light artillery. Very warm today. The 48th Massachusetts Regiment came in yesterday. There are 1,500 strong camped near the hospital. Six regiments are here now.

Sunday, February 23, 1862

Rainy morning, rained hard. No dress parade or drill account of rain. Took squad to wharf in the afternoon. Sergeant Cannon took sick today with dysentery and is very poor. Had preaching here this afternoon by our chaplain. Private Kough got sick today.

Monday, February 24, 1862

Cool morning. Had dress parade. Wrote letter home to Max concerning money sent home. Went to wharf with squad in the afternoon. Not many boats came a shore being very rough. Schooner sunk in the harbor today while unloading coal on a large steamer

Tuesday, February 25, 1862

Very cold and windy. Morning wind blowing in from the sea. Sergeant Cannon is better. Went to work with squad in the afternoon. Mayflower came down from Pinckney Island with prisoners. One with the name of Sherman who used to be in a department here. He was taken for smuggling the government out of goods of all kinds. Very windy at wharf. Boat left today with Negroes.

Wednesday, February 26, 1862

Cloudy and rain this morning. Had dress parade and company drill. Sergeant Cannon no better yet. Private Kough and him taken to the hospital. Went to wharf in the afternoon. Very windy and sea very rough. Rained very hard in the evening. Charles Sherman was caught at Ceylon Island, he was taken for swindling the government store.

Thursday, February 27, 1862

Cool last night and this morning. I was up at the hospital last night waiting on the sick. Sergeant Cannon is no better this morning. Private Kough is better. Had dress and battalion drill. Went to wharf in the afternoon.

Friday, February 28, 1862

Cloudy and warm. Had dress parade and inspection. We were mustered for pay today. Went to wharf as usual. Took two drunk men to their quarters. Ship came in today from New York and brought in Maine's 2 Company of Engineers. The 6th Connecticut came up from Savannah, the men are very sickly is the reason they are brought up here. Two prisoners were brought here today from Beaufort by M. Boone.

Saturday, first day of March, 1862

Cool and rainy. Had dress parade and battalion drill. M. Boone of the 100 regiment stayed in our tent with us last night. Smith and Kemp was going to Beaufort today but there was no boat. Yesterday, the Herrison left here for New York with very large mail. Mail is expected here today. Went to wharf as usual this afternoon. Nothing of importance occurred today. Cool wind in the evening.

Sunday, March 2, 1862

Rainy and cloudy. Had dress parade and inspection at 9am. Went to wharf in the afternoon. Chaplain preached in afternoon here in the new building. Very windy and disagreeable. Today, two boats came in the Mississippi and Matanges. The foreman brought in the largest mail to this office. The Mississippi has on board General Butler. He was on his way to Ship Island at Hatteras Shoals. His ship ran aground and anchor broke and came in here in distress. Mail came ashore this evening.

Monday, March 3, 1862

Cool morning. Had general inspection of all troops on the island. Our company did not turn out-were all on duty. Got letter from Cuz Gwin. Was at wharf all day. Got letter from W.H. Moore. Seen fish 40lbs in weight.

Tuesday, March 4, 1862

Coldest morning we have had in a long time. Ice this morning in small quantities. Second time there has been ice since we are here. This morning got 3 papers from W.H. Moore. Went to wharf in the afternoon. Nothing of importance happened today.

Wednesday, March 5, 1862

Rain this morning. Had no roll call, dress parade, or drill. Wrote letter to Alex Gwin, W.H. Moore and company went to wharf as usual. The 55th PA. Volunteers left here this evening. It is rumored today of the capture of Fort Fernandina on the coast of Florida. The 6th Connecticut was paid today.

Thursday, March 6, 1862

Clear morning. Had lots of fun last night with Private Fred Hench. He was acting corporal in place of Jacob Boyles. He is not well. Went to the wharf in the afternoon very windy and cool.

Friday, March 7th, 1862

Very cool this morning, ice on the pond. Did not sleep well it was to cold. Do not feel well for several days but am able to do my duty. This is the coldest day we have had since we are here. Snowed some. The first snow I have seen since I came on the island or to this state. Did duty as usual. Four steamers came in this afternoon. Atlantic and Oriental (other two steamers were not legible)

Saturday, March 8, 1862

Cool morning. Got letter this morning from J.M.B. of Duncansville, Pa., answered today. Mail went out on the Oriental. Colonel Sernell went to New York and Sergeant Cannon returned to camp from hospital today. Went to wharf as usual.

Sunday, March 9, 1862

Cool Morning. Have no roll call. Had dress parade and inspection of arms. I did not turn out. Took dose of Psalts. Was not safe to go on inspection. Got news yesterday Wm. Burkharts house was burnt on the 27th of February, 1862. Had preaching here today. I was not there being on duty on the wharf.

Monday, March 10, 1862

Windy as usual. Had dress parade and company drill by Sergeant Cannon. He is being able to volunteer duty again. Wrote letter to mother last night. Bought a box of cigars today. Went to wharf as usual. Atlantic is being unloaded. Had lots of fun with cattle. They jumped into harbor and swam out and chased soldiers around camp.

Tuesday, March 11, 1862

Raining this morning. Had dress parade and company went to wharf in the afternoon. Still unloading the steamer Atlantic. Went on board the Westover, a schooner loaded with goods of all kinds. Captain is a very clever man. Bargained for 4 boxes of cigars, came a shore bought 7 fish for $1.10, came to camp, sold 2 fish for $0.50, 2 more for $0.30 and kept the rest. Boys playing tickley [7] this evening.

Wednesday, March 12, 1862

Had dress parade and company drill. Heavy firing was heard in the direction of Savannah. 2 deserters of the Rebel Army were in here today. They report that distress prevails to a great extent in Savannah. Pork is $0.22 per lb. 2 Negro soldiers had been drafted on the 4th of March, 1862. Went to wharf in the afternoon. Rained very hard. Atlantic is not unloaded yet. She had large quantity of Government stores on board.

Thursday, March 13, 1862

Rain and cloudy. Had no dress parade. Sketched a little today. Went to wharf and heard heavy firing towards Fort Pulaski.

Friday, March 14, 1862

Very foggy. Had dress parade at 8:15am and company drill by Sergeant Cannon. Got news today that 2 Rebel boats tried to run the blockade to go to Ft. Puluski but were refused by our boats. Captain Rambo's body and a corporals body of the 45th PA. Vol. was brought here from the other island. They were killed by company K of the same regiment. Mistaking them for the enemy on the night of the 13th at 4am. also wounded 7 men. Captain Rambo is of Columbia, Pa.. This is one of the many deaths which happen this way. Atlantic is still lying at the wharf yet.

Saturday, March 15, 1862

Nothing of importance except mail came in at 7pm. Done duty as usual.

Sunday, March 16, 1862

Clear morning got mail before breakfast. Got letter from Jerry G. This forenoon answered letters. Went to wharf in afternoon. Atlantic left here with mail for New York.

Monday, March 17, 1862

This is St. Patrick's Day. The Irish are celebrating this day as usual with whiskey, heard much cheering in camp tonight. General Sherman left this evening for Fort Fernandina.

Tuesday, March 18, 1862

Clear morning had dress parade and battalion drill by Captain Campbell. I went to the wharf and rushed drill. No commissioned officers on duty. Went to the wharf as usual. Nothing of importance.

Wednesday, March 19, 1862

Cloudy this morning. Had dress parade and company drill by Sergeant Cannon. Went to wharf this afternoon. Nothing of importance took place. Rained at 6pm and thundered very hard. Two pieces of Shermans Battery [8] now called Hamiltons left for Beaufort today. An attack is expected there soon by the Rebel forces. They are now concentrating themselves at Port Royal Ferry where General Stephens brushed them New Years day.

Thursday, March 20, 1862

Rained in the morning. Had no dress parade. Mail came in the forenoon on a steamer that left New York on the 12th. Brought news of no importance. I got no letter in the mail. Do not care 2 cents. Went to wharf as usual, nothing of importance.

Friday, March 21, 1862

Clear morning. Had dress parade and then stacked arms was ordered to fall in at the tap of the drum which sounded at 9am. Then marched up to the regiment, had dress parade and there after had regimental drill. Orders were given to captain to see that each man had forty rounds of cartridges. After dinner went to wharf as usual gun boat came up from Fernandina, Florida. Two pieces more of artillery were sent to Beaufort.

Saturday, March 22, 1862

Cloudy this morning. Sun shown through the clouds for few moments was red as blood. Had dress parade and battalion drill. Went to wharf in the afternoon.

Sunday, March 23, 1862

Clear morning. Had dress parade and inspection. Ship Oriental came in with mail from New York. Got letter from A.R. and W.H.M. and from home. All well. Nothing of importance. Sailor fight at wharf. Cool all day, wind blew from ocean.

Monday, March 24, 1862

Cool morning. Had dress parade and battalion drill by Captain Campbell. Had fun drilling. A marine soldier buried here today. He was of the gun boat Susquehanna. He was shot on duty at Mud River by our own pickets.

Tuesday, March 25, 1862

Cool morning. Had frost this morning here. Wrote to W.H.M. this morning and late night wrote to Fred Yingling.

Wednesday, March 26, 1862

Cool morning and cloudy. Our squad has to go to the wharf at 8am and relieve Company A. Stay till 12pm relieved than by Company A and relieved again at 4pm. Stay till dark. Oriental is still here.

Thursday, March 27, 1862

Went to wharf at 6am and stayed till 8am. Very cool this morning.

Friday, March 28, 1862

Today the steamer Oriental left for New York. Took 50 discharged soldiers home. Daughter of our regiment went home. Says she will be back in twenty days. I hope she never comes back. I believe they are a nuisance to the regiments. Oriental took large mail this evening.

Saturday, March 29, 1862

Clear and warm. Went to wharf at 6am. Went to woods for bush. Got dinner and went back to wharf. Nothing of importance occurred.

Sunday, March 30, 1862

Very warm morning. Went to wharf at 6am. Mail brought in from the Atlantic at 5pm. A mail boat is always welcomed by thousands of sailors on this island. General Hunter is on this boat also Captain Saxon's lady and one other lady. Did not go to the wharf this evening.

Monday, March 31, 1862

Very foggy and warm. This morning went to the wharf. The Atlantic came along side the wharf this morning. I got a letter from C.J. Mitters today and folks are all well.

Tuesday, 1st of April 1862

At home, this is the day to get new neighbors but here it is new neighbors all the time. Atlantic is discharging her cargo. Answered cuz Call's letter today.

Wednesday, April 2, 1862

Very foggy morning. Went to wharf at daylight. News today that there was a Rebel gun boat ran the blockade to Fort Pulaski. Corporal Albert D. Moore got his discharge today.

Thursday, April 3, 1862

Very foggy this morning. Nothing of importance today. Today the 3rd New Hampshire and 8th Maine got marching orders. 3rd New Hampshire to Edesto.

Friday, April 4, 1862

Cloudy this morning and all last night. The 2nd Regiment is leaving here now, hauling baggage to the boat. Albert Moore and Henry Ditch of our company started home. Last night a member of Company I of our regiment shot himself. Supposed to have done it willfully (May have been Private Dennis Curtin from Company I.

Saturday, April 5, 1862

Cloudy morning. 3rd New Hampshire went to Edesto Island today. Part of the 97 PA regiment went to Fernandina. At 4pm General Hunter inspected all the troops on the island. Had a good time.

Second issue state colors of the 76th Pennsylvania Volunteer Infantry.

Sunday, April 6, 1862

T.L. McGlathery and I got passes outside of picket today. Visited Drayton & Eliotts Plantations. Saw nice flowers and had a general nice time in the woods. I always feel glad to get out of our dusty camp as often as possible. 1st Sergeants and musicians got swords today. Company got shoulder straps also had no church as chaplain has gone home.

Monday, April 7, 1862

Warm and clear. Mail came in today. Maltano came in from New York with much news up to the 3rd of the month. She is the prettiest boat here.

Tuesday, April 8, 1862

Cloudy morning. Got one letter from home. A corporal went to the wharf for me today in my place. I have very sore lip which the wind makes them pain me very much. Got medicine from the doctor today. Regiment got orders to march tomorrow at 6am. Companies A and F will not go.

Wednesday, April 9, 1862

Rained very hard this morning. Regiment left old camp at 6am while it was raining very hard. Went on board the boat and left for Tybee Island at 8am. Four of each company was left to guard the quarters. Four families of whites came in today on a gun boat from Florida also 5 Negroes from Edesto Island.

Thursday, April 10, 1862

Clear morning. Last night we went up to old camp and brought down tent frame at 8am the bombardment ceased at Fort Pulaski and since that time we have heard two guns fire.

Friday, April 11, 1862

Clear morning. Firing commenced at Ft. Pulaski at daylight. Shots were fired at intervals all last night but this morning is raging with great fury. This day one year ago the Rebels captured Ft. Sumter from the Union forces under Major Anderson. Today shots are fired at the rate of about 4 per minute. Today Ft. Pulaski fell into our hands after two days of bombardment. Another great victory is won by the loving army of the North. Mail came in today. 3 letters. One from E. White 1 from W.H. Moore 1 from home.

Saturday, April 12, 1862

Very windy this morning. Sand flying as usual. Answered all letters I got yesterday. News this morning that Ft. Jackson was taken last night. Nothing of importance took place today.

Sunday, April 13, 1862

Windy as usual. Do not have any dress parade since Capt. Campbell is Provo Marshall. Had no inspection today Capt. Campbell sick but better today. John Kough and me got pass to go to Tybee Island today but there was no boat. McClelland came up from Ft. Pulaski with 100 prisoners today. They are now being guarded in our camp. I am on guard tonight. Wrote letter to Capt. Wayne today. Got along very well with prisoners. Say they are satisfied. They will be whipped yet. Cooked all last night for prisoners.

Monday, April 14, 1862

Cloudy this morning. Got a small mail yesterday. I got no letter. The one hundred prisoners left here today on board the McCleland for New York. Took 8 days of provisions along with them. Today at 2am got orders to fall in. Company A and F went to the wharf. Went down and brought up 232 prisoners. The 232 prisoners are now camped in our quarters. 50 of the 2nd Rhode Island came to assist in guarding them tonight. Prisoners very contented so far.

Tuesday, April 15, 1862

Clear this morning. Got along very well with the prisoners last night. Today the ship called the Vermont came in. She is a gun boat. Two tiers of guns 84 in number. Today the officers of Fort Pulaski were brought here. There is a very fine cooking officer wears a grey uniform. There is 12 officers. Our company will be all on guard.

Wednesday, April 16, 1862

Cloudy and very warm this morning, rained a little. Got small mail this evening. The prisoners baggage was all searched and all fire arms. We were instructed to be in readiness at a minutes warning as there was some suspicion of an attack by the prisoners tonight.

Thursday, April 17, 1862

Clear and warm all night. 50 of the 97 PA Vol. is here helping us to do guard duty. We got paid today at 2pm. Got 2 months pay which came very handy here now. 160 soldiers and officers of the Rebel Army went aboard the steamer Oriental, 100 left here yet.

Friday, April 18, 1862

Clear morning. Was on guard last night. Got mail this morning. Got letter from Abe Rees and answered them both today. Mail came yesterday on the Atlantic. Very warm today.

Saturday, April 19, 1862

Cool morning. Wrote letter home and sent $20.00. Our regiment came up from Tybee Island today and are camped where the 28th Massachusetts regiment was. Went on guard this evening. Some of the boys are pretty snoozy this evening.

Sunday, April 20, 1862

This is Easter and a pretty day. We had 2 eggs a piece this morning. Lots of fun last night with the fellows. Nothing of importance today.

Monday, April 21, 1862

Cool and windy. Rained at 8am very hard and cleared up at 12:00. News today that the Merrimak was sunk four days ago. Atlantic not here yet.

Tuesday, April 22, 1862

Windy and cool. This morning did not get up till 7am. Alex is sick this morning. Last minute our regiment was ordered to Saybrook near Pinckney Island. Rebels were expected on Pinckney Island to capture our pickets there. The 45th PA volunteered 15 men. Regiment came back at 10am. The Rebels did not make their appearance.

Wednesday, April 23, 1862

Warm morning. Was on guard last night-had a pleasant time. 40 of the 3rd Rhode Island regiment helped us to guard prisoners. Private Frederick Crossman from our company discharged from the hospital by not being able for duty. Will leave here tomorrow on the Atlantic for New York.

Thursday, April 24, 1862

Nothing of importance today.

Friday, April 25, 1862

Warm and cloudy. Moved our quarters today. Camped near the fort on the beach. A very nice place for camp. Company A did all the guard duty today.

Saturday, April 26, 1862

Woke up this morning and found ourselves in a new camp. Our company is doing all the guard duty while Company A moves. Bathed in the bay in the evening. Prisoners still down at old camp.

Sunday, April 27, 1862

Cold wind from the northeast all day. R.M. Bell and me took walk out of breast works today. Eight schooners came in today but no mail yet. Nothing of note took place.

Monday, April 28, 1862

Cool and windy, yet Captain Campbell is moving his quarters today. Five schooners came in today loaded with coal for the port. Engineers would not go to work this morning because they have not been paid but two months pay yet and have been in service 9 months. Dug a well today. Got good water at 12 feet.

Tuesday, April 29, 1862

Warm and pleasant this morning with a sea breeze. Building cook house today.

Wednesday, April 30, 1862

Cool and pleasant. Went on guard today. Today is the day to muster for pay.

Thursday, the 1st of May

Warm as usual. Stayed down at the guard house last night. Had good time. Our guard Richard Bell was on with me. This morning went up to the regiment and was mustered for pay. Came back at noon. Carpenters working at new guard house.

Friday, May 2, 1862

Cloudy morning. R.M. Bell and Marion Smith and I got pass to Saybrook today. Went outside the breast works took straight course through the woods and came out at Stoners Plantation 2 miles southwest of Saybrook. Company F of the 45th PA Vol. is camped there. Got dinner went from there to Saybrook then to Edesto from there down the beach to camp. Had hard time crossing swamp. Got to camp at dusk. Pretty tired. Was detailed at night to go on duty to search for whisky. Found 115 bottles and two Negro wenches sleeping with sailors. This was a pretty busy day and night with me.

Wednesday, May 7, 1862

Cool last night and this morning. Nothing of importance the past few days..

Thursday, May 8, 1862

Cool morning. Went fishing caught nothing. Went in the afternoon Smith caught a small shark. Company B of our regiment went to Saybrook today to relieve a company of the 45th PA and they went to other island to join their regiment.

Friday, May 9, 1862

Pleasant morning. Atlantic came in this morning brought mail and news up to the 6th. Yorktown was surrendered to our forces. Got letter from S.B. and J.H. Gwin. Answered letters this evening.

Saturday, May 10, 1862

Warm morning. Went on guard this morning. Nothing of importance.

Sunday, May 11, 1862

Foggy this morning. Came off guard at 7am was relieved by Corporal Bell. Had to take command of wharf squad again. Corporal M. command was taken from him by the Marshall.

Monday, May 12, 1862

Clear this morning. Went to wharf at 6am. Nothing of importance today. Sergeant Brown went to Drayton Plantation to take charge of the Negro soldiers. Tonight report came in on gun boat that Richmond had been taken and 82,000 prisoners.

Tuesday, May 13, 1862

Warm and pleasant. Nothing of importance.

Wednesday, May 14, 1862

Pleasant morning. Went to wharf as usual. Wrote letters to H. Maurer today. Small steamer came in today from Charleston. She was stolen from the Rebels by a Negro pilot and crew, while white officers were a shore. Atlantic left the dock this evening. She took on board 150 or 200 passengers for New York and other states north.

Thursday, May 15, 1862

Cool morning. Large ship came in last night. This morning a ship came in from Florida. Reports things quiet down there. Sergeant John Boyles was reduced to ranks today for neglect of duty by orders of Colonel Bowers.

Friday, May 16, 1862

Cool morning went to wharf early. Sergeant Cannon, Joseph Kemp, Miles Kinsel, John Moorland is still sick. Large ship from New York came in.

Saturday, May 17, 1862

Warm morning. Went on duty at 8am. This is a very warm morning sun is hot. John Kough, Marion Smith went out to Negro camp. Smith came back Kough stayed out all night. Miles Kinsel was taken to the General Hospital today.

Sunday, May 18, 1862

Warm and cloudy. This morning mail came in on gun boat. Got news to the 14th. Got letter from home and paper-all well. Rained here at 5pm. Sergeant Gwin is sick for a few days past not bad.

Monday, May 19, 1862

Warm morning. 2 Company of the 1st Massachusetts Calvary went to Edesto today also one of the engineers went on the steamer Boston. Have pain in my head. Sun shines hot. Fleas are bad here now also nates and flies are numerous.

Tuesday, May 20, 1862

Warm as usual but cool at night. Very comfortable sleeping. Today our company of Cavalary left for Edesto Island where a force is collecting to advance on Charleston soon. Charleston is 60 miles from here 48 from Beaufort. Fort Sumter will have to be bombarded also Fort Moultrie on the opposite side of the river. No news today. Sergeant Joseph Cannon is sick again. Had a quarter of cured beef but happened not to be good. Sent ring to Anna.

Wednesday, May 21, 1862

Cool very pleasant. A sea breeze blows all day. Marion Smith went to be Orderly Sergeant in the Negro regiment. Engineers gone to Edesto. Also the cavalry went to north Edesto Island. Two companies of the third Rhode Island went to North Edesto.

Thursday, May 22, 1862

Cloudy and warm. Went to wharf at 6am. Changes has been made in our company. Thomas Morgan 5th Sergeant was promoted to 3rd Sergeant instead of Joseph Brown joining the Negro regiment. John Boyles was made Sergeant in place of Joseph Brown being reduced to ranks for neglect of duty by orders of Colonel Powers. A. Crawford Gwin (speaking of himself) was appointed 5th Sergeant in place of Thomas Morgan being promoted. Corporal Henry Miller not being satisfied about Sergeant's Boyles promotion tore off his stripes. Preparation is being made to advance on Charleston soon.

Friday, May 23, 1862

Clear morning nothing of importance today. Still transferring troops to Edesto Island.

Saturday, May 24, 1862

Cloudy morning rained a little today. Heavy firing was heard out about the light ship. Soon a large gun boat made its appearance, then another which was a English Man of War. She had been down at Fort Pulaski last night and then she came up to the light ship fired a salute at 6pm. She fired another salute of 22 guns. Fort Welles on this island returned the salute. This evening Company A and part of our company went up to the regiment to dress parade. Rained this evening.

Sunday, May 25, 1862

(forgot to write)

Monday, May 26, 1862

Our men went to the wharf as usual. Ragan got hurt by a drunken soldier of the cavalry came to quarters all bloody. Put him in the guard house let him out the same day. Last company of the cavalry went to North Edesto.

Tuesday, May 27, 1862

High wind all day and ruff sea. Still looking for mail boat to come in. Reported that the Oriental ran a ground on Cape Hatteras not generally believed. Yesterday evening put two soldiers in guard house for being drunk. were very noisy for a while but quieted down and slept all night. Fleas were very bad. News came in today that the steamer Oriental was wrecked off of Hatteras inlet during the storm on Saturday night and that 2 schooners were taking her freight off. I hope it is not time. Regiment is under marching orders today.

Wednesday, May 28, 1862

Clear and cool morning. Nothing of note. Company B of our regiment came in from Saybrook today. The Rebel steamer Planter[9] which the Negroes ran off with from Charleston City at the wharf. I was on board of her. She is a very neat boat. Carries a 32lb rifle cannon and small howitzer. Had dress parade this evening. I acted as orderly sergeant. Orders from Colonel Brown read 2 men of the 45th Regiment eat dinner here. Company E camped at Spanish Wells.

Drawing of the side wheel steamer Planter, taken by Robert Smalls.

Thursday, May 29, 1862

Very warm some fog this morning. Sun came up with more heat then any morning since we have been here. Steamer General Burnside came in a 9am from New York with 33 boys. Papers confirmed report that the Oriental was wrecked at Hatteras Shores. All the passengers were sent back to New York to take a new start. Regiment had orders to march at 2pm but was countermanded not being able to get transportation. Got letter from home. All is well, dated 19th of May. Drilled squad in the evening.

Friday, May 30, 1862

Clear morning. Answered letters from home. Went to transportation stable to get team to hall slabs. All were being used for building coal yard at Saybrook. Got team in the afternoon. Went to woods for wood. Six companies of regiment left at 2pm. John Kough went with sergeant to camp hospital. Department went out on the Cosmopolitian. Went to North Edesto.

Saturday, 31 Last day of May 1862

Clear and hot sun this morning. Jesse Eyre, prisoner who has been here since January last was taken prisoner while hunting ducks 7 miles below Savannah. He is a Pennsylvanian by birth is being sent to Pa. Companies H & K are going to Edesto to join the other 6 companies. A very small boat came in yesterday with dates up to the 27th. Sewed on sergeants stripes this evening.

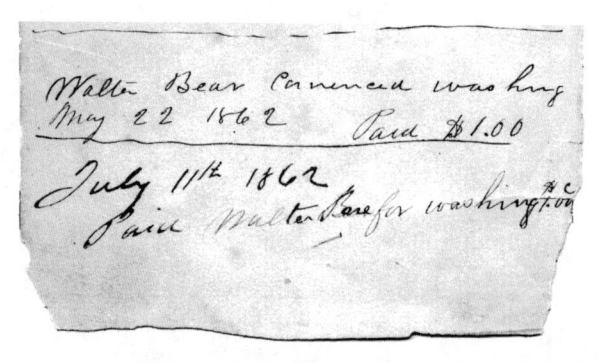

Sunday, June 1, 1862

This is a very warm day. The sun very hot. I am on guard and I lost my knife last night. The six blade one. Company A went to Edesto Island to join the regiment found my knife the same day. Had good lemonade to drink today. Had a good dinner of potatoes in butter Alex is a good cook when he takes a notion. Fleet is now getting ready to go to Edesto Island all are leaving this island but about 12 hundred men. All leaving but the 50th PA. regiment, Calvary Company 2.

Monday, June 2, 1862

Clear morning at 6am. Three guns on the fort were fired. The Erexson came direct from New York with mail up to the 29th of May and passengers of the Oriental which was wrecked on the bar near Hatteras. Captain Wayne of our company and Sergeant Moore came on the steamer. Captain had been absent since the 7th of April. Sergeant had been absent on recruiting service since January 8, 1862. Was very glad to see our old friends back again. Captain and sergeant look healthier now then when they left.

Tuesday, June 3, 1862

Cloudy this morning. Had lots of fun last night. Stayed up last night till 11pm. Had supper at 10pm. Commenced raining at 10am rained all day. Sergeant Morgan on guard today. Sergeant Cannon is getting well again. Rained very hard at night. Tonight a great many visitors to our tent to see sergeant. Upset Sergeant Cannon's ink bottle and spilled all his ink. Did not get scolded much.

Wednesday, June 4, 1862

Cloudy and rain today. Stormed all last night. Slept in the horse stable by myself. The flies bit pretty well did not sleep much. Small mail, got letter from S.B. wrote letter for Sergeant Moore. Captain bought molasses out of company funds. Got to drink cider at captain's tent tonight.

Thursday, June 5, 1862

Cloudy, rained at daylight. Cleared up and sun was very hot all day. Marion Smith who left to drill Negroes 2 weeks ago returned today. Steamer Erexson came in from Stone Island 1 1/4 miles from Fort Sumter. Our men are erecting batteries there. Alex is sick today has something like the fever.

Friday, June 6, 1862

Cloudy morning and very warm. Stayed in camp in the forenoon. In the afternoon went to fish. Caught one and came back at 4pm. Signed the pay rolls. Boat came from Edesto brought mail that was sent up there on Saturday. Got letter from A.D.Moore dated 23 of March. Erexson's cargo is being discharged at the wharf. Alex is better. No letters this evening. No news from Edesto.

Saturday, June 7, 1862

Clear this morning. Went on guard. Fleas were not as bad last night. Slept well. Large steamer seen lying outside the bar this morning. Rained at 10am. Corporal Miller is on guard with me at 1pm. Steamer came in, proved to be the Aurora direct from New York with mail dates up till the 3rd. News of an advance made by McClellan, Fremont and others. Got letter from Corporal C.J.M all well. Alex was taken to the hospital. Has been sick for 5 days past. Rained and stormed very hard. This evening heard today that our regiment was on Johns Island-are now in Gen. Williams Brigade formally Col. of the 12th Massachusetts Cavalry.

Sunday, June 8, 1862

Cloudy and very cool. Had to wear over coat. Had good time on guard last night. Came off at 8 this morning. Wrote letter to cuz C.J.M. Slept 3 hours today. Rained hard at 12pm. Went to hospital to see Alex this evening. He is getting better. One man died in the hospital today. Tent leaked very much today. Sergeant Moore is out tonight with payroll at Negro quarters. Fleas very bad tonight.

Monday, June 9, 1862.

Very windy this morning. Rained some in the forenoon. Sergeant Moore on guard today. Last night a patrol went to Negro quarters and brought up 8 soldiers 4 of Company A and 4 strangers. Kept Company A in guard house all night. Private Smith returned to the company a few days ago. We had him mustered in today. Again Sergeant Moore and I found him to be an unable bodied soldier as usual. He is now a member of this company as before. Went to hospital in the afternoon, found the sick all getting better except Joseph Kemp who appears worst. Wrote letter for Corporal Hughs

Tuesday, June 10, 1862

Windy and cool this morning. Did not sleep well last night fleas were very bad. Smith and me scrubbed are tent out today. Alex is better today. News today the pickets of the 48th PA regiment had a brush with the Rebels last night on Dawfaski Island did not hear the result.

Wednesday, June 11, 1862

Warm this morning. The steamer Benj Safford came in last night from New York. Left New York on Sunday at 4pm. Had small mail received in camp at 5pm. Nathan Brown got box of cake which I had the pleasure to help eat. One cake had a paper around it read, "two bites for a hungry soldier and another one of the receiver of this will please send a box of shells." Maggie Anderson

Thursday, June 12, 1862

Clear morning. Boat came from Edesto today brought Maj. Wright from James Island also a Rebel officer. Wrote letter to Isac Maurer. Got jacket bound by tailor in company. This evening Sergeant Cannon and me took walk down to the beach came back at 10pm. Capt. Campbell sick today and Rebel prisoner brought in today.

Friday, June 13, 1862

Clear and very warm. Sun very hot in the morning. Did not get up till 7am. Today at 2pm Company A was paid. Company A went home on furlough. There was about 300 passengers on board.

Saturday, June 14, 1862

Cloudy morning. Got paid at 9am. Private got 26$ each. Had great time getting clothing requisitions signed by Col. Brown. I drew provisions for company. Bought sheep liver for 25 cents.

Sunday, June 15, 1862

Cloudy this morning. Had a good breakfast of liver. Had inspection. Went on guard. Very warm day. Firing is heard. At 9am the steamer Vanderbuilt came in and 3 schooners came here for the 1st Massachusetts Cavalry to take them to Richmond.

Monday, June 16, 1862

Cloudy and very windy. Had heavy storm at 3am last night. Fleas and other insects very bad. Slept from 2am till morning. Sergeant Moore went to woods for wood for prisoners and got very wet. Bought ham for $1.82 cents. Had good dinner. Alex returned from hospital today almost well again.

Tuesday, June 17, 1862

Rained this morning. Strong wind from the east. Steamer Locust Point arrived here at 5pm this afternoon from New York with news to the 13th of June. Had small mail. Rained so hard the cooks could not cook supper.

Wednesday, June 18, 1862

Cloudy morning. Cleared up at 9am. Mail came in from the gun boat Rhode Island. Cosmopolitan came from Edesto today. Reports that a fight took place on James Island on Monday. Loss was heavy estimated at 1000 killed and wounded. Our regiment lost 6. Got letter from cuz E. Snyder. Visited the hospital. Sick all getting better.

Thursday, June 19, 1862

Clear and windy. Corp. Bell went to woods for wood. Rained hard at 4pm. Steamer Beydeford came from James Island with 300 sick and wounded soldiers. John Kough and James Stewart came back. Report is now that about 700 of our soldiers killed and wounded and taken prisoners. Tonight at 10pm ambulance are running to and from hospital. Today Col of 48th New York regiment died here very suddenly from infection.

Friday, June 20, 1862

Clear morning. Ambulances still hauling wounded from steamer. Two men died last night one of our regiment at 2pm. Today steamer Erexson arrived from Key West. 7th New Hampshire regiment and Company E of the 1st US Artillery are stopping here tonight.

Saturday, June 21, 1862

Clear morning. Went on guard this morning. Steamer came from New York today with mail. I got no letters. Rumors today that last night a gun boat came in with news that Richmond is taken.

Sunday, June 22, 1863

Cloudy, came off guard at 8am. Had inspection. Last night had fun and trouble with John Shannon who was Corp. on guard with me. He got drunk. He and John Kough had a few words and then he hit him. Shannon is a disagreeable man when drunk. Small steamer came in from Hampton Roads. Took walk to wharf this evening.

Monday, June 23, 1862

Clear. Quite stressing time here today. Two Hundred wounded soldiers went on board the Erexson which left here at 5pm. Company 5 from the 47th PA came from Key West.

Tuesday, June 24, 1862

Clear and warm this morning. Got ten passes. A squad of men went to saw mill and got 2 loads of slabs to build sink. Had fresh beef for dinner.

Wednesday, June 25, 1862

Cloudy morning. Got up at 7am and cooked breakfast. Soldiers caught big fish weighed 1300lb harpooned it called a devil fish. Sergeant M and me went up to see sick and wounded soldiers. All getting along well. One man died last night from wounds in the shoulder.

Thursday, June 26, 1862

Clear morning. Went for fresh beef at sunrise. Had some for breakfast. Alex went on guard the first time since he was sick. Steamer came in at 5pm from New York-mail to the 23rd. Did not get any mail until 10pm. I got no letter from home in 2 weeks.

My Opinion in arming Negroes & drilling them as soldiers.

In the first place I ask the person who first hinted at making soldiers of the Negroes & putting them on an equality with the white soldiers. In answers to the above question I say that it is contrary to the constitution and the regulations of the army of the united and which a direct insult to our Government and the 76.

And in the next place it has a tendency to show to other nations that the Loyal States of America are weaker than first Represented by the Union people of the North and will also show to the world that the Rebellion States are stronger by far than first represented by the Northern States. When this rebellion first broke and the call was made for soldiers to suppress the Rebellion but how different is it now when we hear the order of the General Commanding our division of the Northern Army proclaim freedom to all the slaves in & of the Southern States in which he has hardly footing enough to camp his troops is not this contrary to the Constitution and acts of congress. I say it is because this war is not intended to free the Negroes-to suppress the Rebellion is what these soldiers left their Families and came here to sacrifice their lives for. Abraham Lincoln & his cabinet are on the right track now if they only continue. So I say. Slavery & freeing the Negroes are one thing and Suppressing this Rebellion is another. And I think uncle Abe & I agree. Sergt. A Crawford Gwin Written June 28, 1862 at Hilton Head Island, South Carolina

My Opinion on arming Negroes & arbing them as Soldiers

In the first place I ask the Rson who first wanted of making Soldiers of the Negroes & putting them on an Equality with white men. Answer to the Question I Say that it is contrary the Constitution and the Regulation of the army of the United and contrary to the Act Passed in our Government the Sitting of 76—

And in the next place it had a tendency to Show to other nations that the Loyal States of america are weaker than the first Refused by the Union and also of the South and will also Share to the doute that the Rebellion States are Stronger than First Refrenced by the Southern States. the Rebellion has not B K and the Cote now Make for Soldiers to—

When this Rebellion first broke out they wanted to their troops in one generating of a rebellion ane rather than wanted the War to end & to a General Out come it wanted ts — more over then the Southern Army Broke Smaller to support Commencing one Division — to the Northern army to all the Slaves to be of the Southern States to which the whole better than this all the Slaves to be of the Southern of which the hundredly for any enough to carry their troops to not this Contine two to the Constitution and act of Congress for it — is because this War is not intented to free the Negroes but Support the Rebellion a what they Listen doft their People one can here to Subdue the laws for Abraham Lincoln & his Cabinet — an the right track now If My act Copy and two Days & Nights or Selling & Killing of the Man John Brown and and a Jages

Written June 28/1862 at Hillers Head South Carolina for two mos
Saml S. Cranford knin

Friday, June 27, 1862

Clear morning. Went on guard at 8am. Corp. Hench is on with me. Mail came in at 10am on gun boat. I got one letter from home. All well. Two prisoners were going to fight yesterday in the guard house. This is very troublesome duty acting Provo Guard.

Saturday, June 28, 1862

Very warm and sun hot this morning. Came off guard at 8am. John Kough cut my hair. Mail came in got no letter.

Sunday, June 29, 1862

Cloudy morning. Had no inspection today. Corp. Bell and me took walk on beach. Private Jacob Hackenthorn of Company A died today at 10am. He was buried at 5pm. I went to funeral grave yard-is about 1/2 mile from town. Two men from our regiment died today. Heard today that all the soldiers on James Island and our regiment were coming back here to Beaufort.

Monday, June 30, 1862

Clear and warm. As today is one of the days when the soldiers mustered for pay, we got ready, packed our knapsacks had inspection and mustered for pay by Capt. Campbell. Got box from home. Was out at 47th regiment got some nice shells. Four boat loads of soldiers came from James Island this evening

Tuesday, July 1, 1862

Clear and warm. Got up at 5am went on guard at 8am. Company had drill according to orders of yesterday evening. Had good time on guard. Police brought in drunk man. Wrote letter home. Ocean Queen left here yesterday.

Wednesday, July 2, 1862

This is a very warm morning. This morning one year ago today the 3rd PA regiment of 3 month soldiers crossed the Potomic where I first set my foot on the soil of the Old Dominion [10]. That was the day when the battle of Falling Water was fought and the Rebels defeated. The day was just about as hot as today. The Arago sailed at 1pm. Capt. Campbell went home on furlough. Arago took 50 wounded soldiers home.

Thursday, July 3, 1862

Very warm. Sergeant Moore on guard today. Went with squad to wharf. This forenoon 8 Maine regiment left here for Beaufort. Today thunder and lighting very hard. This evening Col. John M Powers came here from James Island. Joseph Kemp of our company died last night in the General Hospital and was buried today.

Friday, July 4, 1862

Cloudy very quiet this forenoon. At 12am national salute at Fort Walker. Good many drunk soldiers. Guard house filled at 5pm. B.Difford came in with 100 regiment Pv. from James island. George Boone is with us tonight. This fourth was spent with me as last fourth. We can not tell where we may be next fourth. J. Trover of Company A was buried today at 5pm.

Saturday, July 5, 1862

Cloudy morning very warm. Last night was cool-slept well. Sergeant Morgan on guard today. Nothing of importance took place. Rumors that the Provo Guard is to join the regiment tomorrow.

Sunday, July 6, 1862

Cloudy this morning. News this morning that we are to join our regiment at 10am. Had orders strike tents while striking tents 2 Company of 3 New Hampshire regiment relieved us. Got moved up to regiment by dark. Mail came this afternoon on Exerson had dates to the 2 of July. No news of importance. Have very nice quarters here more shade trees on our street.

Monday, July 7, 1862

Clear morning. Got up very early this is my day to cook. This is a very warm day. Drawed 4 day rations and the Provo Guard requisition turned out in dress parade with regiment. We have a very nice place to camp. Have shade trees in street. Beach was filled with soldiers this evening sunning-drilling and on lookers.

Tuesday, July 8, 1862

Nothing of importance took place today. Wrote letter to Isaac today.

Wednesday, July 9, 1862

Clear morning got up at reveille. Had no roll call. Went on guard at 3pm had review of all the troops on the island on Draytons Plantation. At 5pm our regiment said to be the largest one on parade. Some of the soldiers were sun struck. One man of the 45th Pv died on the field.

Thursday, July 10, 1862

Clear morning. Was a nice night to be on guard. 100th regiment left last night for Beaufort. The Vanderbuilt came in this morning. Got cloudy and windy at 9am. I slept on top of Company H's cook house. Man of Company G was buried yesterday at 4pm died in General Hospital.

Friday, July 11, 1862

Clear morning slept well all night. Yesterday the steamer came from Boston-called the Mississippi with news from Richmond. McClellan had been driven back 15 miles. 6 regiments are leaving here to join McClellan's army. Today our company sent all the articles of clothing which they did not need. I sent all home that I did not need. Had a heavy storm of rain and wind this evening. Daniel Reagan member of this company died in General Hospital this morning of bilious fever.

Saturday, July 12, 1862

Cloudy morning. Daniel Ragan was buried this morning at 9am half of company turned out. He is buried in a very nice grove of pines where all the soldiers are buried that died here. When we came back from funeral signed the pay rolls and at 1pm was paid got $32.12. Alex bought fish and sold them. News that McClellan has taken 8,000 prisoners.

Sunday, July 13, 1862

Clear morning. Had regiment inspection on parade ground. A man by the name of Dalrimple in Company A was buried at 5pm.

Monday, July 14, 1862

Nothing. I got no letter. Do not know what Susy is about-she does not write.

Tuesday, July 15, 1862

Nothing of note today.

Wednesday, July 16, 1862

Very warm this forenoon. Cooler in the afternoon. Had dress parade as usual. At 6pm. orders from war department concerning sick and each regiment to send them home to their own state from each regiment .

Thursday, July 17, 1862

Warm morning Sergeant Gwin went on picket guard. I kept house for him was drawing picture of General Hospital. Corp. Bell and me went down to dock in the evening. Rumor that Richmond was taken.

Friday, July 18, 1862

Cloudy and warm this morning. 45th Regt. Pv went on board Arago. 97th Pv came here on the Delaware at 12am. Steamer Arago and Delaware left other dock and steamed out to sea. I guess the are bound for Fort Monroe. Sergeant Moore on guard today.

Saturday, July 19, 1862

Clear morning and very warm. Mail came in on gun boat. Got letter from Max one from C.J.M. Was working on pictures of hospital here.

Sunday, July 20, 1862

Cloudy morning. Had inspection in camp by our own officers. Two regiments came in from Edesto Island this afternoon. Alex and me went down to dock saw M. Detwiler and Will Krise. Rained this evening at 6pm had no dress parade in that account wrote letter to Max Gwin. Sergeant Moore not well today has yellow jaundice.

Monday, July 21, 1862

Clear morning and warm as usual. Did nothing of account. Read in Robison Caruso. Had dress parade this evening. Will Knox is very sick. This evening today a Negro struck a soldier with an axe he is not expected to live. General Hunter is not the man. After this I wish he would be removed. Another Negro killed a sergeant of the Provo Guard and two soldiers killed the Negro.

Tuesday, July 22, 1862

Clear morning. This morning one year ago I was lying sick in General Hospital at Hagerstown, Maryland. 3 month soldiers were on their way home.

FEDERAL ZOUAVE

Wednesday, July 23, 1862

Clear and sun hot. Will Knox took to hospital this morning he is very sick. Private of company A died last night. Was buried at 5pm this afternoon. Alex was very sick to day with colic. Sergeant Moore still has jaundice yet. Walter Bare has quit washing for company.

Thursday, July 24, 1862

Warm and clear. Marion Smith and me went to dock this morning. Negro market was crowded very much. Lots of melons and chickens. Steamer Boston came in from New York this morning. News to Sunday the 20th. No news of importance.

Friday, July 25, 1862

Awful warm this morning. Went on guard at 7am. Steamer McClellan came in at 8am from New York with mail. Read papers to the 21st. No advance has been made on Richmond yet. Thermometer at 117 in the shade at 11am. This is the warmest day we have had yet.

Saturday, July 26, 1862

Warm as usual. Was released at 8am today. Negro market was very much crowded. This morning mellons, figs, peaches, and all kinds of vegetables. Plenty of fowls of all kinds. Will Knox is very sick today. Not expected to live.

Sunday, July 27, 1862

Cloudy morning and very warm. Had inspection of arms and quarters. At 8am 30 Negroes were baptized. Had sassafras tea for dinner today. Will Knox very bad today. This was as pleasant an afternoon as we have had since last fall.

Monday, July 28, 1862

Cool and pleasant. Nathan Brown and me took walk down to the beach at sun rise very pleasant. Marion Smith went to Negro market but no boats came in. Will Knox died today at 8am. Took furlough to Col. Williams to get forwarded to Gen. Hunter but Hunter would not sign it.

Tuesday, July 29, 1862

Warm morning as usual. Buried Will Knox at 8am. Marshall band was present. He is buried near a thorn bush. Steamer left today for Fort Monroe at 1pm. General Wright and staff went on board.

Wednesday, July 30, 1862

Nothing of importance today very warm. A man of Company E was buried today. Mail came in today on the Mississippi.

Thursday, July 31, 1862

Warm this morning at 8am good sea breeze. One year ago I got home from 3 months service. Today I was to sick to walk.

Friday, 1st day of August 1862

Cloudy and very warm got up at 5am. Report read at dress parade that a rebel steamer is going to run out of the Savannah river and brake the blockades here and 8 other places. We all got more cartridges this evening.

Saturday, August 2, 1862

Cloudy morning no rain came last night. Firing was heard towards Ft. Pulaski. Today Company A has 40 on guard. The guard is to be detailed by companies now. Regiment had drill this evening our company was not out. Preparations were being made to receive the Rebel blockade runner. Rifle cannons are being mounted on the fort here. Walter Bare and me took walk to woods. Got some sassafras root and found some grape vines. Came back to camp had tea for supper which was very good. Sergeant Moore and me took walk to wharf in the evening.

Sunday, August 3, 1862

Cloudy and warm had no inspection this morning. 43 of our company went on guard I was on at Gen. Hunter's quarters. Got very wet. Rained hard in the evening

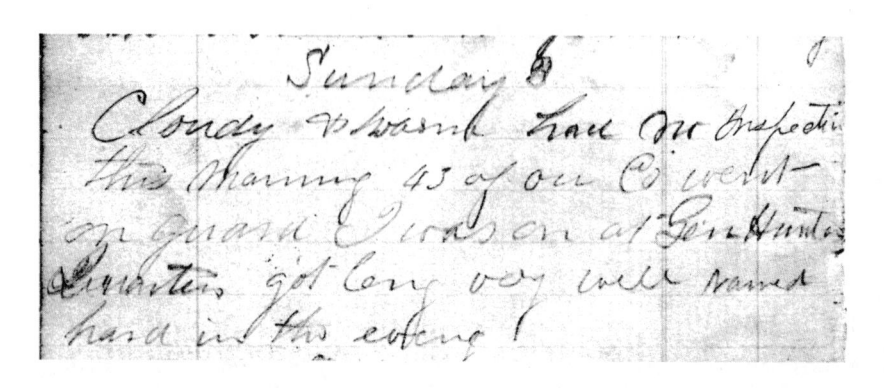

Monday, August 4, 1862

Cloudy morning. Came off guard at 8am. Large party of soldiers and Negroes working on breast works and pulling trees outside to prevent Rebels from advancing on us here. Steamer Arago came in last night with mail. I got no letter. No news of any importance. John Shannon of our company is going home. He is discharged on account of disability.

Tuesday, August 5, 1862

Clear morning. Star of the South left at 4am this morning. 10 men on fatigue duty today along with the rest. Worked pretty long all day. Got whisky in the evening. Regiment out of meat. Received barrel of pork today.

Wednesday, August 6, 1862

Clear and warm. No detail of our company expected. The steamer run this afternoon did not come.

Thursday, August 7, 1862

Cloudy and very warm. 38 of our company on guard this morning. Had great time in camp today. Jack Williams of another company was to be bucked and gagged[11] for refusing to do his fatigue duty. Sergeant went to gag him and soldiers would not let it be done. Then Col. Powers ordered all company under arms and then tied him. Sergeant Boyles of our company read the charges and he will be court marshaled. Williams was sent to the Provo. Guard. Thermometer 104 degrees.

Friday, August 8, 1862

Cloudy morning almost like all mornings are now. Wabash came in this morning from New York with mail. No news of importance. Got letter from home all well. Thermometer 95 degrees. Camp guard put on at 5pm this afternoon by orders from head quarters. 24 of our company 10 who were out last night and out tonight. Hard duty at present.

Saturday, August 9, 1862

Clear and warm. 34 of our company on Post Guard. Co G on fatigue duty. Jack Williams refused to do duty. and was to be bucked and gagged. Some of all the companies turned out and had a big time. Jack got over to our company we all were ordered to fall in and then Jack was tied and was arrested and taken to Provost Guard.

Sunday, August 10, 1862

Warm as usual. Nothing of importance except Col. Powers having resigned and went home on the Arago which left here at 5pm today. It is expected that Capt. D.C. Strawbridge will be Major of this regiment. Companies C.H.F. on extra duty for 11 days for disobeying orders during the bucking and gagging of Jack Williams.

Monday, August 11, 1862

Warm as usual. 33 of our company on post guard. 63 of company on fatigue duty in the afternoon. I was not on duty. Thermometer 109 degrees in the shade.

Tuesday, August 12, 1862

Rainiest Monday we have had yet. Thermometer 90 degrees am 110 degrees in the shade in pm. Got book from New York today called "Advice to Young Men". Our company is not on duty today. The first day we have not been on duty for ten days past.

Wednesday, August 13, 1862

Clear and very warm this morning. Thermometer 110 degrees in the sun. 53 of our company on fatigue at 4 and half o'clock this evening. The squad I was in had no spades and we did not work and came back to camp. The rest worked till 8 and 1/2 o'clock PM. Wrote letter home today. Mail to leave on gun boat today.

Thursday, August 14, 1862

Cloudy morning. Nothing of importance took place.

Friday, August 15, 1862

Clear morning. Went on guard at 7am at camp. Salute was fired in honor of Ex President Van Buren who died at Sandybrook, New York on the 20th of July last 1862. A gun was fired every half hour all day and at noon. A national salute was fired on Fort Walker. Boat came in from New York with small mail I got no letters. News that a fight was going on in Richmond.

Saturday, August 16, 1862

Cloudy this morning rained some last night. Guards slept in quarters last night. Capt. A. Hamilton officer of the day in camp of 76th. Saw a water spout this morning. Very pleasant night. 32 of company F went to work on fort at 5pm. I went to post office.

Sunday, August 17, 1862

This is the coolest morning we have had since April last. Wind blows very hard and cool. Sergeant Warren Moore and 3 Corporals and 40 men of our company on police guard today. Steamer Star of the South came in from New York at 10am. No mail brought. News that General Pope has whipped Rebel General Jackson near Richmond. Cool in the evening. Can not sleep well. Slept 5 hours today.

Monday, August 18, 1862

Clear and cool. Our company came of guard this morning. Nothing of importance today except a gun boat came in at 4pm fired a salute of 12 guns. Believe it was an English vessel. Wabash returned the salute.

Tuesday, August 19, 1862

Cool morning. Guards had to wear overcoats on duty. Is very cool at this time of year especially in this climate. Joseph H. Hughes of our company got in a fight.. Massachusetts Cavalry is going on board the boat and all the transports are lying here ready to go. No detail out of our company today. Will catch it tomorrow.

Wednesday, August 20, 1862

Rained hard last night and is raining at sunrise this morning. 48 of our men on guard today. Thomas McGlathery and I went to dock today. English gun boat came in today. Fired a salute-Wabash returned the salute. Calvary regiment left today for Fort Monroe. Col. takes command today. Col. Williams went with regiment to Virginia.

Thursday, August 21, 1862

Cloudy morning. Company came of guard. Doing nothing today. Major Irwin is sick. Nothing of note occurred today.

Friday, August 22, 1862

Cloudy and some fog this morning 44 of our company on guard police today. S.S.M Sergt. today in place of J.A.B. Rained hard this morning cleared up at 8am. At 1pm Corp. Miller and I were detailed to go out on fishing expedition. Went out on beach found two sailors they had caught plenty of Rock Hearing. We helped fish awhile with them came into camp with about 2 bushels of fish. Company has plenty. Henry Burkholder was taken to the General Hospital sick with fever. J.H.H came back today.

Saturday, August 23, 1862

Clear morning. McGlathery was on guard last night. Today we got new hats about 2 feet high red color. Great fun with them. Today we looked for the Arago but she did not come. Have not had a mail for a week past. Did not hear from home since 17 of July. This evening 9pm Henry Burkholder of company died in camp hospital of inflammation. Had been sick for 7 days. He was on detached service in Quartermasters Department.

Sunday, August 24, 1862

Cloudy morning went on guard at 8am. 32 of our company on duty today. Capt. a. Hamilton officer of the day in camp Capt. Young officer of day in Breast Works. Henry Burkholder was buried at 5pm in soldiers grave yard outside fort beside William Knox of this company.

Monday, August 25, 1862

Cloudy and rainy since 5am. Slept from 2:30 till 6:00 this morning. Came of guard at 7:30. No mail yet. Arago did not come in yesterday. Policed in forenoon and afternoon. Mowed weeds and grass in front of color line. Going to move camp make one row of tents instead of 2.

Tuesday, August 26, 1862

Cloudy rained hard last night. At 3pm tent leaked. Gun boat Connecticut came in at 1pm with mail and papers to the 23rd. No news of importance. Commenced striking tents and moving. Rained hard at 3pm did not get much done. Got mail at 8pm. I got no letters. Slept in orderlies tent on moss tonight.

Wednesday, August 27, 1862

Rained hard last night. 45 men of our company is on post guard today. Rained hard this afternoon got all the tents up. Got new tents put up few of them.

Thursday, August 28, 1862

Cloudy rained hard this morning. At daylight worked on tents until 12am. We then got orders to be ready to march on Saturday 30th at daylight.

Friday, August 29, 1862

Clear morning went to fix up awning in front of tents. If we do leave here will come back again in 7 days. Review at 4pm today by Major General Hunter. Had nice time got through at dark. Came in camp and took a hearty supper. Got new men yesterday George Giboney and John Detwiler. They are both nice boys so far.

Saturday August 30, 1862

Clear morning got up at 5am. According to orders given in the evening formed on parade ground to march. Do not know where. Stood in line awhile and then marched to quarters and our company and Company A went on guard. So much for marching orders.

Sunday, August 31, 1862

Cloudy morning. Company came of guard at 7am got ready for mustering. Call beat at 9am found on parade ground had inspection of arms. Mustered two companies and it then commenced raining. Marched to quarters. 4 hours later cleared up-finished mustering and inspected knapsacks and tents, cook house and company. Captain Strawbridge of Company B now commanding regiment was the mustering officer. Had no dress parade. Sergeant Moore is not well.

Monday, 1st Day of September 1862

Clear with a few flying clouds. Our company is not on duty today. Company went to woods for poles to finish awning in front of tents. Steamer Star of the South came in this morning from Fort Monroe. Brought no news or mail.

Tuesday, September 2, 1862

McClellan came in today also gun boat Susquehanna with large mail but no late dates.

Wednesday, September 3, 1862

Cool morning. Got our mail this morning got letter from S.W. & A.C.

Thursday, September 4, 1862

Cool this morning. Answered a few letters. Went to Post Office. Massachusetts came brought news that Gen. Pope had defeated Jackson and Lee near Marcuss Junction. I got no letters.

Friday, September 5, 1862

Was on fatigue all day. Steamer St. Maye came from New York brought dates to the 1st of September. News that Pope had whipped Jackson's Army at Bull Run. A old battle ground of 1861. Got ready this evening to go to do picket duty on Pinckey Island. Gen. Hunter and staff left for Washington this evening at 5pm.

Saturday, September 6, 1862

Cloudy morning. According to orders our regiment got ready. Call was sounded at 5:30am and all formed on parade ground. Then started for Graham's Plantation 6 miles from here on the northwest side of the island. 2 companies went to Seabrook. Our company and company A went to the Spanish Wells. This is called the Spanish Wells as there is 2 wells of very good water. Looks like something they have in Spain. It is the best water on the island. We relieved 2 companies of the 97th PA Volunteers.

Sunday, September 7, 1862

Clear morning. Got up early went to farmhouse which is 1 mile further on the banks of the Broad River. From here we could see the mainland and Ft. Pulaski. Can see the rebel town of Bluffton.

Monday, September 8, 1862

Cloudy morning. I went with squad of 10 men to open big mail.

Tuesday, September 9, 1862

Nothing of importance today.

Wednesday, September 10, 1862

Clear morning and did not sleep much last night. Mosquitoes very bad. Sgt. Ferguson went to Fort today. Boat came in today with news that rebels were near Washington - don't believe it. No mail.

Thursday, September 11, 1862

Clear and warm. Went on picket this morning at 8am. Had good time generally.

Friday, September 12, 1862

Clear as usual. Very pleasant last night. This morning at daylight seen men leave Bull's Island had thought it was rebel spies but it proved to be contraband Negroes coming from Bluffton and Hardyville 18 miles from here. They say there is no rebels near there. Came of guard took Negroes to Col. Guip who is commanding post now - came back to camp.

Saturday, September 13, 1862

This morning at 9am was relieved by 2 companies of the 7th Connecticut Volunteers. All night very windy- sand and dust flying very much . Very disagreeable. Got letter from A.G.G. Sgt. Moore is getting well.

Sunday, September 14, 1862

Cloudy rained hard last night and today at 9am had no inspections. Rations scarce today.

Monday, September 15 1862

Cloudy morning rained hard at 8am . Heard there is to be 3 hours of drills each day. Company drill in forenoon and battalion drill in afternoon. Arago came in at 1pm with mail with dates to the 12th. News that the rebels are in Hagerstown Maryland in strong force. Gen. Mitchel came to take command of this department which was to be called the 10th Army Corps. General addressed the regiment on the misfortune of not having field officers here to command it. He gave our regiment praise for its fine appearance. Concluded by saying we had work to do down here and as soon as government would aid him he would commence to move on mainland. He also said he would make our regiment as it once was one of the first regiments in service. General is fair and hardy looking and looks to be 50 years of age. Has a firm voice and determined look. Speaks with ease and to the point.

Tuesday, September 16, 1862

Cloudy and windy morning. Got our mail, I got letter from home dated August 24. Answered it today. Had company drill this forenoon. Had no battalion drill. Capt. Strawbridge not well.

Wednesday, September 17, 1862

Cloudy and cool. Nothing of importance took place.

Thursday, September 18, 1862

Clear morning. Went on camp guard at 8am. Mail came in on gun boat this morning. I got no letters. Had good time on guard. Sergeant Marshall was officer of the day in camp of the 76th regiment.

Friday, September 19, 1862

Cloudy, cool and pleasant. Came of guard at 8am. Had review and inspection of the troops at 11am.

Saturday, September 20, 1862

Cloudy and warm. Rained small showers in forenoon. Had no drill. Walter Bare very sick today. Warren Moore is not any better today. More sickness in our regiment today then any other day since our regiment came out. Rained this evening.

Sunday, September 21, 1862

Took sick with Chills and fever.

Wednesday, 1st of October, 1862

Did not take any notes while sick. On one day there was 45 who took sick. Nothing of importance took place the last ten days except yesterday small expedition left for Jacksonville, Florida. Got letter from home yesterday. Wrote home to J.S.G. Today is warm.

Thursday, October 2, 1862

Cloudy morning. Mail came in this morning on Star of the South with papers to the 27th. No news of importance. I got no letters. Capt. Wayne better.

Friday, October 3, 1862

Cloudy morning. Wrote letter to cuz Bill and M. Kough. Mail went out today on the Star of the South at 5pm. Feel well today. Sick all getting better.

Saturday. October 4, 1862

Cloudy morning. Nothing of importance. Today went on dress parade this evening. Had not done any duty since 22 of September. Will go on duty tomorrow. Was said on dress parade that we are now in the first brigade, commanded by Brigadier General Tesey, formerly Colonel of 7th Connecticut Vol. Brigade consisted of 97th and 76 Pa. Vol. 7th Connecticut and 3rd Rhode Island Vol. Very pleasant. Sergeant Gwinn on picket. Sergeant from Company H who was court marshaled for both conduct and drunkenness was released today and returned to duty.

Sunday, October 5, 1862

Clear and warm this morning. Went of guard down at fort. Had good time.

Monday, October 6, 1862

Cloudy, did not sleep any last night. Came of guard at 9 am. No news today except that the small fleet that left here last week captured Jacksonville in Florida and some artillery on the 3rd of the month.

Tuesday, October 7, 1862

Warm, nothing of importance today. Had battalion drill at 4pm by Capt. Strawbridge. No mail yet. Two men in tent got very drunk. Say they always feel worst afterwards.

Wednesday, October 8, 1862

Cool last night and cool morning. No post guard out of our regiment no picket. Only 20 men on camp guard. For the last month our regiment has been furnished 150 guards each day. You would think we would have a few days rest now which we need. Sergeant Moore is no better yet. All other sick getting better.

Thursday, October 9, 1862

Cloudy morning. Nothing of importance.

Friday, October 10, 1862

Cloudy, cleared up at 8am. Had no drill. Orders came at 5 pm for detail of 44 best men in company to be ready to march at once

Saturday, October 11, 1862

Nothing of importance today.

Sunday, October 12, 1862

Cloudy and rained today. Do not feel well have chills and fever. Mail came in at dark.

Monday, October 13, 1862

Cloudy morning rained hard last night was very sick and did not sleep. Feel better this morning. Today the 400 men that was detailed for the expedition were put into 8 companies. 50 men in each company. Companies I & K were broken up. Mail at 12pm. I got no letters. Had battalion drill in the afternoon.

Tuesday, October 14, 1862

Cloudy morning. Gun boats shelling Bluffton on the mainland. Today reported that 500 rebels are there. Steamer left for New York at 4pm. Had battalion drill.

Wednesday, October 15, 1862

Cloudy as usual. Steamer Mississippi came in this morning and news that Rebels had been in Chambersburg, Pa. and destroyed some railroad property there and was retreating towards Virginia. Had company drill in the forenoon. Got socks and shoes today. Had battalion drill.

Thursday, October 16, 1862

Clear morning. Had drill in forenoon and battalion drill in afternoon and dress parade. Nothing of importance today. Joseph Cannon and I took walk down to the beach this evening. Very pleasant. I am getting well again.

Friday, October 17, 1862

Cloudy morning. Had company drill in the afternoon and battalion drill. Warren H. Moore 2nd Sergeant of this company got his discharge today for disability. Has been sick for 2 months.

Saturday, October 18, 1862

Cloudy morning and very cool. Nights are now getting cool and winds blowing from the east. Had company drill as usual. I was at dock, did not drill. No battalion drill this afternoon. Expedition is being set out to make an attack as soon as the rebels reach the mainland.

Sunday, October 19, 1862

Clear morning. Had inspection in quarters. Wrote letter home to Max. Nothing of note today.

Monday, October 20, 1862

Clear as usual. Regiment is preparing to leave. Four in our company was taken to General Hospital today.

Tuesday, October 21, 1862

Clear morning. Had orders to be ready to march at 12:00. When the time arrived we left camp and went to wharf. Two companies went on board a steamer and the balance on the Flora-a fine little boat. Stayed on boat all night which lay in the harbor till 2pm. When the fleet left it consisted of 5 transports and 8 gunboats. Number of men 4500. At daylight, found us 12 miles up the Broad River and at 8am came to McAry's Point. This is a part of land between Pocotaligo and the Broad River. All got ashore and started inland. Marched five miles and we heard artillery firing in front of us. We commenced double time and soon were near the fight. We laid undercover till the artillery made the rebels "skidaddle". Very heavy cannon fire on both sides. Here the 47th Pv lost heavily. Our regiment was now in advance and soon artillery was engaged again. Soon we came up to them. Our regiment was first. We pitched right in and fought till night. Commenced about 2am. We then got orders to fall back which was done in good orders. We came to McAry's Landing and the night of the 23rd got back to Hilton Head. Those killed in our company: Captain Henry Wayne, Private William Boyles, Private Adam Fry, Sergeant Gwin and 7 more wounded. From the 24th to this date, I have been sick with fever and vomiting. Feel better today.

Tuesday 21th 1862

Clear Morning had orders to be ready to March at 12 Oclock, when the time arrived we left Camp went to warf & Co went on board the Steamer Called Water Wich and the balleance on the Flora a fine little boat — Stayed on boat all night which lay in hubor till 2 P.m. on the 22. when the fleet left wh consisted of 5 transports & 8 gun Boats No of Men 45.00 at daylight found us 12 Miles up the Broad River and at 8 A.m. Came to McAys Point o point of land between Pocataligo & Broad River all got a shore and Started in land March Marched 5 Miles and we heard artiley firing in front we Comenced Double and soon were near the fight lay under

Cover till Artilery Made the
Rebels Skedaddle very heavy Canon-
-ading on both Sides here the 47
P v lost heavy Our Regt was
Now in advance and Soon Artiley
was engaged again in front
Soon we came up to them ours
was the first Regt on the ground
we Pitched right in and fought
till nights Comenced bout 2 P.m.
we then got orders to fall back
which was done in good order
Came to McAys Landing Same
Night and the Night of the 23
got back to Hilton Head
From the 24 to this date the
27 I have been Sick with
fever and vomiting feel better to
day. 28 29 29. 30 Nothing of
Importance I am not fit for duty
yet a few cases of Yellow feaver
is here Now Gen Mitchels Son
has it Capt Waifield of Mitchels
Staff died with it

October 28, 29, 30, 1862

Nothing of importance. I am not fit for duty. A few cases of yellow fever is here now. Gen. Mitchel and son have it. Captain Waifield of Mitchel's staff died of it.

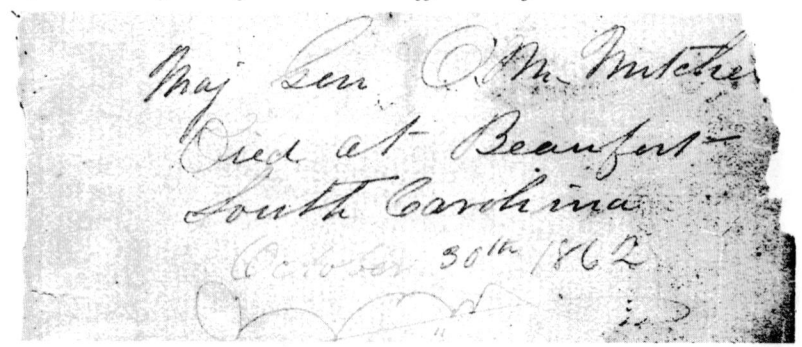

> Maj Gen O.M. Mitchel
> Died at Beaufort
> South Carolina
> October 30th 1862

Friday, October 31, 1862

Clear and cool. Had inspection and mustered for pay. Now have 4 months pay. Heard today the Major Gen. Mitchel died at Beaufort yesterday evening at 6pm of yellow fever. Flags are at half mast and a salute was fired from the Wabash at 11am in honor of Gen. Mitchel. Not many cases of yellow fever yet. Was mustered today as 4th Sergeant.

Saturday, November 1, 1862

Cloudy and cool. Nothing of importance today. Yesterday evening at 7pm Corporal Frederick Hench of our company died in regiment hospital of fever. Was buried today at 3pm. Star of the South left for New York at 5pm. Private George Gibboney got box from home today. Everything in it was nice.

Sunday, November 2, 1862

Cloudy and cool. Nothing of importance today.

Monday, November 3, 1862

Cloudy and warm. Had regiment drill this afternoon. Building new hospital. George Gibboney and Graham Meadville sick in quarters and I am acting hospital steward. 21 of our men are sick. I washed all my clothes today.

Tuesday, November 4, 1862

Cloudy and cool. Wind blowing hard last night. Men still sick, but better.

Wednesday, November 5, 1982

Steamer came in from Key West Florida. Had no drill today.

Thursday, November 6, 1862

Rainy this morning. Rained hard last night. Slept in Pvt. David Kounsman's tent last night. Had coffee for dinner today. Nothing of importance.

Friday, November 7, 1862

Last night very cool. Slept well. Pretty day today. One year ago this place was taken from the rebels. A national salute was fired at 12am, also at one half past 4pm by the Navy. This is the time the rebels surrendered. Cool evening.

Saturday, November 8, 1862

Cool morning. John Delaney died last night at 10pm. Was buried at 3pm. Today along with balance of the 76th Pv took down awnings in front of tent. Got new overcoats today.

Sunday, November 9, 1862

Cool morning. White frost - the first we have had this fall. Went on guard at 8am. Nothing of note today.

Monday, November 10, 1862

Frost this morning again. Was cool on guard duty last night. Came off at 8am-was relieved by Sergeant of Company C. Took good sleep after dinner. Went on battalion drill at 3pm. Got supper - feel badly. No mail yet. Had none since 20th of October.

Tuesday, November 11, 1862

Clear day. Built house in front of our tent today. Makes quite an addition to tent. Graham Meadville got box from home today. All things nice.

Wednesday, November 12, 1862

Warm morning. Cut hair today. J.S. Kough commenced washing for company this week. Henry Buel went to General Hospital today. Has typhoid fever. Cpl. Hench's mess broke up today. Cloudy evening.

Thursday, November 13, 1862

Clear day. Had chills and fever today. Doctor gave me quinine and rehuibart. No news from North yet.

Friday, November 14, 1862

Cloudy morning. Feel better- slept well last night. Gibs working on tent floor. Meadville on guard. Firing on gunboat and forts today, practicing I suppose. Not well today.

Saturday, November 15, 1862

Was not well yet this morning. Took Emetic. Vomiting very hard till noon. Started to throw up blood. Was taken to General Hospital in the evening. Stayed there till Friday, November 21st. Was then able to come to quarters. Got mail on the 18th- a month since last mail.

Saturday, November 22, 1862

Windy and cool all day. I am staying with Sgt. Gwinn now. Nothing of importance today.

Sunday, November 23, 1982

Cool morning. Very cool last night- slept well. Had inspection today. Col. complimented us on a good appearance of quarters. Had potatoes dinner. Sgt. J.R. Findley was here last night all night. He is now at the Spanish Wells.

Monday, November 24, 1862

Cool morning. Pretty day. Mail came in this morning on steamer City of Richmond and Cosmopolitan. Got letter from home dated Nov. 16th. Answered it today. Graham Meadville sick today. No news of importance. William Burkhart went to General Hospital today. Cool evening.

Tuesday, November 25, 1862

Clear morning. Got up early. Have roll call 3 times per day. Wrote letter to Frederick Yingling, Allegheny Mountaineer, Cambria County, PA. Steamer Delaware started for New York today. Had no battalion drill.

Wednesday, November 26, 1862

Cloudy and cool today. Fixed up stove today. Made one out of camps kettles. Does first rate for a stove. Had potatoes cooked on it.

Thursday, November 27, 1862

Clear day. Very pleasant. This is Thanksgiving Day in Pa. Also the day Brig. Gen. Saxon of this state has appointed officers on this island. Went to Fort Pulaski today to have some fun. Boys here enjoyed themselves playing and company as well as could be expected. G.G. and G.M.M. had a small knockdown today. Both came up best of the least. No one was hurt.

Friday, November 28, 1862

Clear and cool. Officers came up from Fort Pulaski today - say they had a good time.

Saturday, November 29, 1862

Clear and cool as usual. Stood sentinel for George Gibboney from 10 to 12 pm last night. Last night got good drink of brandy. J.H. Sulter went on guard . Had good time all day. Had dress parade at 4pm. Orders read that a man of the 9th Maine Regiment is to be shot here the first of December in presence of all the command here for desertion and going to the rebels at Florida , C.S.A.

Sunday, November 30, 1862

Cool morning but pleasant day. Came of guard at 8am. Had regiment inspection at 9am. Was excused from it - had no dress parade. Had ham for supper and breakfast.

Monday, 1st of December, 1862

Warm an cloudy this morning. As this was the day for the execution of a man of the 9th Maine Regiment who was named and tried for desertion at Florida in June last. He was sentenced to be shot in presence of this command. Early in the morning, preparations were made and all the regiments marched outside of the Breast-works and formed in a hollow square opened at one side. And at 11am the hearse made its appearance escorted by 50 of the 47th New York Volunteers commanded by Major VanBurst, Provo Marshall of this place. The prisoner was seated in the hearse when they arrived in the center of the square and halted. The prisoner got out of the wagon himself and walked to the place where he was to be shot guarded by two of the pall bearers. Without arms, a coffin was then taken to him and he sat down on it. Charges of his trial was read to him. He then stood and spoke as follows: "Fellow soldiers, I want you to take warning by my words and seek salvation of the Lord before it is too late. I am not guilty of the crime for which I have been condemned to death."
The following lines he handed to the printer:

Hilton Head, South Carolina, 1862

I am about to suffer death which punishment I am willing to bear for a warning to others which may be led astray by bad company. Fellow soldiers, you should take warning by me and keep of bad company and shun everything that is bad. Keep good company and you will be respected by your worst enemies. Oh may God bless the officers of the Forty-Seventh New York Regiment. They have done everything within their powers and they brought me back to religion and religious papers that led me on the right road to my savior. Oh! May God help and sustain them throughout the peril of the battles.

That they may come out victorious in them all and may God speed the time when peace shall once more be, and the friends that are here at war will be going home to their families.
          Albert W. Lunt [12]
     Once let down again, was then ordered to take his position behind the coffin, kneeling on the coffin in a half-stupped position. Provo Marshall tied a white handkerchief around his head. Two preachers then went to him, had prayer, one standing on each side of him. They went away and 12 soldiers which was standing in line about 12 paces in front of him took aim and at 28 minutes past 11 o'clock, the guns went off and he fell forward over his coffin struck by all the balls of which pronounced him fatal. He did not move a limb after falling. Was dead in two minutes. Was then put in the coffin and put in the wagon and took back near the graveyard and buried. No persons along but the pall bearers. So ended the life of a traitor. No honor due to him. This should be a warning to all soldiers never to betray their trust or desert to the enemy. For desertion in time of war is always punished by death. We returned to camp hoping we had all learned a lesson we never should forget. He seemed resigned to his fate. Was either a Christian or an awful bad man. Mail came in today - no news of importance. Got letter from W.H. Moore.

Tuesday, 2nd of December, 1862

Clear morning. Had company drill in forenoon. Nothing of importance. Signed clothing account today. Did not draw any sugar or candles yesterday. Have none in commissary-none on island. Waiting for troops. A little out of sorts without sugar.

Wednesday, December 3, 1862

Cloudy morning. Nothing of importance. Sgt. McGlathery policing in camp. Him and Sgt. Joseph Canon went out of Fort Mitchel on the northwest side of the island on Scull Creek.

Thursday, December 4, 1862

Cloudy, foggy and cool. Rained a little by the time Sgt. Joe and McGlathery got back today from Fort Mitchel. Cool evening. Stove smoked very bad. Five sailing vessels came in this afternoon.

Friday, December 5, 1862

Nothing of importance today. Had battalion drill. Missed drill this forenoon.

Saturday, December 6, 1862

Cool last night and high winds. Cleared this morning- was eclipse of the moon this morning. This evening, one year ago, our regiment went on board the steamer Illinois at Fortress Monroe, Virginia. This took Captain Wayne's effects to express office, also B.F. Steiner, Frederick Hench, John Delaney, to send them to the families. General Hunter is coming here again. Got barrel of molasses this evening.

Sunday, December 7, 1862

Cool morning, very pleasant today. John Kough and Daniel Devine took walk down to the beach - had nice time. Nothing importance today.

Monday, December 8, 1862

Heavy frost this morning. Went on post guard at fort. Had Sergeant of Company K on guard. Had good time with him. Cool evening. Steamship came in towing a boat. One of Gen. Banks fleet which is reported lying outside of the bar sailing south.

Tuesday, December 9, 1862

Heavy frost as usual. Ice one quarter inch thick in bucket. These are long nights sitting by a firing all night as the guards have to do here on post guard. Guard at 8:30am. Cooking good and wash felt better. Battalion drill in afternoon.

Wednesday, December 10, 1862

Pleasant morning. Steamer left this morning. Sergeant McGlathery on camp guard. Company drill in the forenoon. Dress parade in the evening. Officers of the 114th New York were pleasant. Thought we could not be beat drilling.

Thursday, December 11, 1862

Pleasant morning. Star of the South and 3 other steamers in today. Small mail on Star of South. I got no letters. Had company and battalion drill. Working at Fort Mitchell. Relieved today.

Friday, December 12, 1862

Clear and warm. Wrote letter to S.W. Nothing of importance today.

Saturday, December 13, 1862

Pleasant-warm and clear. 2 Companies of the 9 month Vol. belonging to Mass. 42 Regt. came in here today. Do not think much of 9 month men. Star of South left this evening at 5pm for New York with mail.

Sunday, December 14, 1862

Clear and warm. Nothing of importance except 42 engineers of the 46 New York regiment that was sent to fort in May last- for refusing to work anymore without pay. 23 have agreed to go to work and take their pay. Some of Banks fleet came in today for coal.

Monday, December 15, 1862

Warm and cloudy. Nothing of note.

Tuesday, December 16, 1862

Cool and windy all day. Had no drill. Sand blowing very much. Looking for mail on the Delaware.

Wednesday, December 17, 1862

Windy and cloudy as usual. Had company drill in forenoon. Battalion drill in the afternoon. Boys have plenty of apples today. Was on Post Guard last night. Got them by slight of hand.

Thursday, December 18, 1862

Windy and cool all day. News that Frederick City is taken by Burnside.

Friday, December 19, 1862

Heavy frost this morning. Had company drill and battalion today. Looking for mail on the Delaware. John Detwiler came from Gen. Hospital yesterday.

Saturday, December 20, 1862

Pleasant day. Mail came in today on gun boat. Sent-got-letter from home.

Sunday, December 21, 1862

Cool and windy all day . Stayed in camp all day. Corporal Bell appointed to Sgt. today in place of J.M.

Monday, December 22, 1862

Went on guard today. pleasant and warm all day. News today that Burnside defeated at Fredericksburg.

Tuesday, December 23, 1862

Came of guard this morning. Cool last night-warm today.

Wednesday, December 24, 1862

Nothing of importance. Today wrote letter to W.H. Moore.

Thursday, December 25, 1862

Christmas Day. Warm and pleasant all day. Had potatoes and cabbage for dinner. Mail came in today on the Star of the South. Got no letters. Spent the day playing ball.

Friday & Saturday December 26, 27, 1862

Nothing of note. Brig. General Seymore Cerre on Star of South. Is to be military Governor of South Carolina in place of General Saxton.

Sunday, December 28, 1862

Cool day. Some clouds. Very quiet today. Nothing of importance.

Monday, December 29, 1862

Cool and windy all day some clouds.

Tuesday, December 30, 1862

Cool and windy all day. Boys practicing wheeling barrel blindfolded for match that is to come up on New Years Day.

Thursday, 1st Day of January 1863

The performance in camp today was as follows. First shooting match 3 men from each company. Company B came of best. Running hurdle race. One man from each company. John Boyles of Company F came of the best. Next came the sack race. One man from each company. Man from Company J came of best. Afternoon wheelbarrow race. Company K came of best. Next climbing greased pole. With $5.00 on top of it. No one got to the top of it. Last was contrabands diving in tub of meal for half dollars. This was equal to anything I ever saw for fun. Over cakes and cider were served in abundance also several times through the day beer cider was served to the men. I think this was one of the happiest New Years I spent. The officers of the regiment deserve credit for treating the men so well.

Friday, January 2, 1863

Clear and pleasant this morning. Today Sgt. Gwin on picket. Mail came in yesterday on gunboat- I got no letters.

Saturday, January 3, 1863

Cool day, nothing of importance.

Sunday, January 4, 1863

Pleasant day. Had Company inspection. Quarters inspected by Colonel and staff. Cloudy in afternoon. Major Dillin had dress parade yesterday evening. Did not get along very well.

Monday, January 5, 1963

Cloudy, rained some last night. Post guard today.

Tuesday, January 6, 1863

Cloudy morning. Went on picket at 8am. Rained at 12 pm very hard. Cleared up in afternoon.

Wednesday, January 7, 1863

Cool morning. Had good time on guard last night. Guard rounds came around at 1pm, was relieved at 8pm. Today the 47th New York Regiment came to camp by 10am.

Thursday, January 8, 1863

Cool and windy this morning. Pleasant day.

Friday, January 9, 1863

Clear morning. Star of the South came in this morning with mail. Got letter from A.R. Gwin, J.S. Atland, John Yingling. No news of importance.

Saturday, January 10, 1862

Cloudy morning. Rained hard at 10pm. Wrote letter.

Sunday, January 11, 1862

Pleasant morning. Got rest of new uniform.

Monday, January 12, 1862

Clear and very warm. Man of company died in hospital yesterday and was buried today. Had battalion drill this afternoon. Was at church this evening. Had a good meeting.

Tuesday, January 13, 1863

Pleasant and clear all day.

Wednesday, January 14, 1862

Cool and pleasant. Played ball in the forenoon and battalion drill in the afternoon. Small mail today our company got one letter.

Thursday, January 15, 1863

Nothing of importance today.

Friday, January 16, 1863

Cool day. Windy all last night. Rained hard at midnight. Rained all day today. 97th PA. Vol. came from Helena Island yesterday. Our company took coffee to company G.

Saturday, January 17, 1863

Cool and windy all day. Played ball. Had no drill or dress parade.

Sunday, January 18, 1863

Very windy all day. Steamer came in at 5pm. Maj. Gen. Hunter came on her to take command of this department. Again salute was fired on the fort for him. Brought small mail.

Monday, January 19, 1863

Cool and windy as usual. Mail this morning. I got no letter.

Tuesday, January 20, 1863

Very disagreeable day. Very windy and cool. Nothing of importance.

Wednesday, January 21, 1863

Pleasant morning. Storm is again over. Had company drill in the forenoon. Played ball.

Thursday, January 22, 1863

Clear morning. Went on camp guard at 8am. 9 of Company A and F played ball this afternoon with 47 New York boys. New York boys beat us 2 rounds.

Friday, January 23, 1863

Clear morning. Came of guard at 8am. Had review by Gen. Hunter outside the breast works. Had good time. Star of the South came in with mail and commissions of Capt. J.R. Findly, Sergeant G.H. Gwinn and Joseph Cannon. 16 in all for regiment. Boys in good humor. I got no letter as usual.

Saturday, January 24, 1863

Had general inspection by Capt. Jackson USA and Sergeant Kissly MSA. Was pleased with appearance of regiment and company.

Sunday, January 25, 1863

Foggy day. Got balance of new uniforms today. Preaching today by chaplain of the 47th New York Vol.

Monday, January 26, 1862

Clear day. Uniforms issued today.

Tuesday, January 27, 1863

Rained some all day. Very disagreeable all day.

Wednesday, January 28, 1863

Cool and windy. Snowed a little last night. First snow we have had this winter. I was appointed Orderly Sergeant of Company F 76th PA. Vol.

Thursday, January 29, 1863

Cool and windy. Regiment was reviewed today.

CONCLUSION

This was the last page of A.Crawford Gwin's diary. Most likely he stopped writing at this point having used up his first book. As you can see his daily entries were dwindling near the end.

All records indicate that A. Crawford Gwin was killed at the battle of Fort Wagner on July 18, 1863. Below is the newspaper article from his home town of Altoona, Pennsylvania which reported the battle.

Altoona Tribune
Tuesday, July 21, 1863
STORMING OF FORT WAGNER

In the engagements attending the advance, the 76th behaved most nobly, winning the admiration and praise of Gen. Brannon, the other officer in command, but it suffered severely in killed and wounded. A letter received a few days since by Dr. W.R. Findley, from his son, 1st Lieut. Jos. R. Findley, of company F, gives the following account of the engagement and the loss of that company:

"I have just returned from a point about 13 miles up Broad River, where I have been with an expedition which started from this place on the evening of the 21st. The object was to cut off the rail road communications between Charleston and Savannah. At the place where the attack was to be made, the railroad crossed an island in Broad river, and on each side are large bridges. The gunboats were to destroy one bridge, and the land force, the other. I was attached to the gunboat Water With, as Signal Officer". "The forces landing at the lower point of this land at daylight on the morning of the 22nd. They consisted of the 76th, and the 47th P.V., the 3rd New Hampshire, and parts of some other regiments. *After the troops had advanced some miles, they met the rebels in the woods, and drove them back-when they took position behind a swamp, having previously destroyed the only bridge across it. Our forces at once deployed and attacked. The 76th supported the marine battery on the left of the line, and at the point nearest the rebel lines. Their guns were finally silenced, but our troops could not cross to drive them out".*

"*During the fight several of our men were killed. Capt. Wayne was killed by a shell, which carried away his right arm and part of his right breast. He never spoke after being struck. Capt. Hamilton, Company H. was also killed-shot between the eyes by a rifle ball. I learned from some that the bodies of Capt. Wayne and Hamilton were buried-from others that they were left on the field. If the latter, nothing shall be undone to recover them, especially our own Captains.*"

"*The Blair County boys have again distinguished themselves. They fought nobly and never flinched. The 76th has shown that her number (76) will not be disgraced and have proved itself to be a hard fighting regiment. They stood manfully to their work, and never faltered, till the order to retire was given. The name of Capt. Henry Wayne will now be added to Blair County's sons, who have voluntarily offered up themselves, upon the altar of their country and for the preservation of the Union. Company F is badly cut up-only 18 men being able to answer to their names-although many, it is supposed, were exhausted and would be for some time; also, that many were in the hands of the enemies as prisoners. Orderly Sgt. Crawford Gwin is among the missing.*"

END NOTES

1) **Fatigue duty:** manual or menial labor, such as barracks cleaning assigned to soldiers.

2) **Provost guard:** a detail of soldiers on police duty under a Provost Marshall.

3) **Quartermaster:** a military officer responsible for the food, clothing and equipment of troops.

4) **Fort Wells:** the improved Union version of what had been Fort Walker, a Confederate Fort, prior to the Union takeover.

5) **Drayton Plantation:** Although there was more then one plantation in the area owned by the Drayton family, the one mentioned in the diary was most likely the Drayton Plantation located on Hilton Head Island.

6) **Provo Marshall:** the head of the Military Police

7) **Tickley:** a game played by soldiers where lice bugs were placed on a flat pan over a fire and the last bug to jump off would win.

8) **Sherman's Battery:** Brigadier General Thomas West Sherman along with Commodore Samuel Francis Dupont was in charge in leading the Union amphibious assault on Port Royal Sound, South Carolina. Battery refers to an emplacement for one or more pieces of artillery.

9) **C.S.S. Planter:** the name of the ship that Robert Smalls and the other slaves, including wives and children of the married slaves, began their courageous flight to freedom. Smalls who had ten years of experience working on ships, put on the Captains hat, and at each harbor post, gave the proper salute on the whistle. After passing through fort Sumter they got up a full head of steam, lowered the Confederate flag, and raised a bed sheet as a symbol of truce to any Union vessels. Smalls became a hero when he reached Charleston Harbor. Smalls went on to become a pilot for the navy and thereafter he became the first African-American Congressman, and noted statesman.

10) **Old Dominion:** refers to the state of Virginia.

11) **Bucked and gagged:** a form of punishment in which a soldier's hands would be bound in front of him and his knees shoved up inside his arms and a stick wedged between his elbow and the back of his knees. A gag would then be placed in his mouth.

12) **Albert W. Lunt:** member of the Ninth Maine Regiment. Lunt along with seven other soldiers from his regiment were under orders to stand guard at Judge O'Neal's house located in Fernandina, Florida. On April 7th, 1862 Private Albert Lunt, deserted to the enemy's lines, and reported to the enemy that this party of men was stationed at Judge O'Neal's. On Thursday, April 10th, Captain Baker sent two men to order the party in, who found the dead body of one man, and the remainder of the party taken prisoners.

COMPANY "F" ROSTER

Name	Rank	Muster In	Remarks
Blanck, Jr., William	Captain	11/21/61	Prom. to 1 Lt. Mar. 1, '65; to Capt. June 30, '65 -- Must. out July 18, '65
Findley, Joseph R.	Captain	11/06/61	Prom. to Capt. Oct. 22, '62 -- Disc. Oct 4, '64
McDivitt, James H.	Captain	07/16/63	Drafted-Prom. to 1 Lt. Jan. 3, '65; to Capt. Feb. 17, '65 -- Resigned May 27, '65
McGlathery, Thomas L.	Captain	10/28/61	Prom. to 2 Lt. June 20, '64; to Capt. Jan. 2, '65–Killed at Ft. Fisher Jan. 15, '65
Wayne, Henry	Captain	11/06/61	Killed at Pocotaligo Oct. 22, '62
Gwinn, George H.	1st Lieutenant	10/28/61	Wounded at Pocotaligo Oct. 22, '62 -- Prom. to 1 Lt. Oct. 23, '62; to Brevet Capt. & Brevet Major Apr. 13, '65 --Must. out Nov. 28, '64
Cannon, Joseph W.	2nd Lieutenant	10/28/61	Prom. to 2 Lt. Oct. 23, '62 -- Disc. Apr. 1, '63
Hubert, John	2nd Lieutenant	10/28/61	Prom. to 2 Lt. Apr. 19, '65; . June 13, '65 -- Must. out July 18, '65 Com. 1 Lt
Morgan, Thomas	1st Sergeant	10/28/61	Must. out Nov. 28, '64
Null, James M.	1st Sergeant	07/13/63	Drafted -- Prom. to Corp. Mar. 6, '65; to 1 Sgt. May 1, '65; Com. 1 Lt. July 1, '65 -- Must. out July 18, '65
Boyle, George	Sergeant	01/01/64	A.W.O.L. at must. out
Boyles, John A.	Sergeant	10/28/61	Died at Charleston July 20, '63
Detwiler, John H.	Sergeant	01/01/64	Absent, sick at must. out
Fogel, Peter	Sergeant	10/28/61	Must. out Nov. 28, '64
*Gwin, Alexander R.	Sergeant	10/28/61	Killed at Ft. Wagner July 18, '63
Gwin, James A.	Sergeant	10/28/61	Disc. Surgeon Certif., date unknown
Hurlbert, Lucius A.	Sergeant	03/27/63	Drafted -- Disc. June 28, '65
Kine, William	Sergeant	10/28/61	Disc. Surgeon Certif., date unknown
Miller, William	Sergeant	02/01/64	Prom. to Sgt. Mar. 11, '65-- Must. out July 18, '65
Moore, Warren H.	Sergeant	10/28/61	Disc. Oct. 18, '62
Shay, John	Sergeant	08/27/63	Drafted -- Prom. to Sgt. July 1, '65; Com. 2 Lt. July 1, '65 -- Must. out July 18, '65
Barker, Augustus	Corporal	07/18/63	Drafted -- Must. out July 18, '65
Bell, Richard M.	Corporal	11/06/61	Killed at Drewy's Bluff May 14, '64
Benton, George R.	Corporal	02/22/64	Prom. to Corp. July 7, '65 -- Must. out July 18, '65
Chubb, Thomas	Corporal	03/03/65	Prom. to Corp. July 7, '65 -- Must. out July 18, '65

*Should be written, Gwin, Alexander C. **not** (R.) as in original company roster.

Name	*Rank*	*Muster In*	*Remarks*
Clark, Daniel	Corporal	11/08/61	Disc. Nov. 7, '64
Evans, Charles	Corporal	11/06/61	Prom. to Sgt., Co. K, date unknown
Hinkson, Enock	Corporal	11/08/61	Killed at Ft. Wagner July 15, '63
Hughes, Joseph H.	Corporal	10/28/61	Killed at Chesterfield Heights, VA, May 7, '64
Irwin, Adie F.	Corporal	10/28/61	Must. out Jan. 12, '65
Kinsel, Miles	Corporal	10/28/61	Killed in action July 9, '64
Lafferty, John	Corporal	10/28/61	Must. out Nov. 5, '64
Martin, John W.	Corporal	10/28/61	Killed at Chesterfield Heights, VA, May 7, '64
McCormick, James	Corporal	11/06/61	Prom. to Sgt. Major, date unknown
McCullough, Nicholas	Corporal	07/16/63	Drafted -- Disc. May 24, '65
McKenna, George	Corporal	07/09/63	Drafted -- Prom. to Corp. Mar. 6, '65 -- Must. out July 18, '65
McLaughlin, John	Corporal	10/28/61	Disc. July 13, '62
Miller, Henry A.	Corporal	10/28/61	Must. out Nov. 5, '64
Moore, Albert D.	Corporal	10/28/61	Disc. Surgeon Certif. Apr. 4, '63
Moore, David	Corporal	10/28/61	Disc. Surgeon Certif. Apr. 4, '62
Morrison, Able	Corporal	08/26/63	Drafted -- Prom. to Corp. May 4, '65 -- Must. out July 18, '65
Rockwell, John	Corporal	02/21/65	Substitute -- Prom. to Corp. June 7, '65 -- Must. out July 18, '65
Rutter, Henry	Corporal	07/16/63	Drafted -- Prom. to Corp. Mar. 6, '65 -- Must. out July 18, '65
Snyder, George	Corporal	08/26/63	Drafted -- Wounded at Darbytown Rd. Oct. 27, '64 -- Must. out July 18, '65
Walker, Cornelius	Corporal	10/28/61	Killed at Ft. Wagner July 11, '63
Wicker, Casper	Corporal	10/28/61	Must. out Nov. 28, '64
Knox, John M.	Musician	10/28/61	Killed at Cold Harbor July 1, '64
Long, William W.	Musician	10/10/64	Substitute -- Must. out July 18, '65
Ritter, John	Musician	10/10/64	Substitute -- Must. out July 18, '65
Stewart James G.	Musician	10/28/61	Must. out Nov. 28, '64
Wayne, Jr., Henry	Musician	10/28/61	Must. out Nov. 28, '64
Adair, William S.	Private	10/02/63	Drafted -- Died at Salisbury Nov. 27, '64
Atwell, James E.	Private	08/27/63	Drafted -- Disc. June 22, '65
Ayers, James M.	Private	10/28/61	Must. out Nov. 28, '64
Ayers, John J.	Private	10/28/61	Must. out Nov. 28, '64
Back, Trevanian	Private	10/28/61	Must. out Nov. 28, '64
Ball, William W.	Private	08/27/63	Drafted -- Disc. June 9, '65
Bare, Walter	Private	10/28/61	Must. out Nov. 28, '64
Bartlebough, Henry	Private	10/28/61	Died at Hampton, VA June 29, '64 of wounds rec. in action
Barton, Bright H.	Private	02/26/64	Must. out July 18, '65
Beaver, Levi	Private	10/19/64	Substitute -- Must. out July 18, '65
Berker, Frederick	Private	08/23/63	Drafted -- Must. out July 18, '65

Name	*Rank*	*Muster In*	*Remarks*
Bishop, John S.	Private		Trans. from 203 PA Vol. June 22, '65 -- Absent, sick at must. out
Black, John W.	Private	02/13/65	Substitute -- Deserted March 11, '65
Bollinger, John	Private	07/14/63	Drafted -- Wounded at Darbytown Rd. Oct. 27, '64 -- Must. out July 18, '65
Boyles, William	Private	10/28/61	Killed at Pocotaligo Oct. 22, '62
Bowser, George W.	Private	02/27/64	Absent, sick at must. out
Bradley, Thomas	Private	03/28/64	Died June 12, '64 of wounds rec. in action
Brown, James	Private	02/24/65	Substitute -- Must. out July 18, '65
Brown, James B.	Private	10/28/61	Killed at Cold Harbor June 6, '64
Brown, Joseph	Private	10/28/61	Must. out Nov. 28, '64
Brown, Nathan	Private	10/28/61	Must. out Nov. 28, '64
Broyles, Jacob	Private	02/27/64	Must. out July 18, '65
Buel, Henry G.	Private	10/28/61	Killed at Ft. Wagner July 11, '63
Buffamoyer, Daniel	Private	02/15/65	Substitute -- Must. out July 18, '65
Burkhart, William	Private	10/28/61	Must. out Nov. 28, '64
Burkhart, William D.	Private	10/28/61	Must. out Nov. 28, '64
Burkholder, Henry	Private	10/28/61	Died at Hilton Head Aug. 23, '62 -- Bur. Rec. Sept. 2, '62
Chittenden, Abel S.	Private	09/23/64	Drafted -- Died at Wilmington, NC May 14, '65
Clemo, Stephen	Private	09/23/64	Drafted -- Absent, sick at must. out
Cochran, Michael	Private	02/25/65	Substitute -- Must. out July 18, '65
Cogsdale, Tyler	Private	08/27/63	Drafted -- Disc. July 8, '65
Conners, John	Private	10/28/61	Disc. Surgeon Certif., date unknown
Conrad, Henry	Private	12/23/64	Drafted -- Must. out July 18, '65
Cooper, Isaac	Private	02/15/65	Substitute -- Must. out July 18, '65
Crossley, Matthias	Private	02/21/65	Substitute -- Died July 21, '65 -- Bur. in Cypress Hill Cem., L.I., NY
Crossman, Frederick		Private	11/28/61 Disc. Surgeon Certif. Apr. 21, '63
Daniels, John	Private	10/16/61	Deserted Oct. 17, '61
Delaney, John	Private	10/28/61	Died at Hilton Head Nov. 8, '62
Dell, Samuel	Private	02/22/64	Absent, sick at must. out
Devine, Daniel W.	Private	10/28/61	Must. out Nov. 28, '64
Diehl, William H.	Private	02/17/65	Substitute -- Disc. June 30, '65
Ditch, Henry	Private	10/28/61	Disc. Surgeon Certif. Apr. 4, '63
Dole, Daniel	Private	02/18/64	Substitute -- Disc. June 19, '65
Dunham, Joseph	Private	08/25/63	Drafted -- Disc. June 12, '65
Faiven, Martin	Private	02/21/65	Substitute -- Must. out July 18, '65
Finley, Stephen	Private	08/27/62	Killed at Ft. Wagner July 11, '63
Fleck, Luther E.	Private	10/28/61	Died at Hampton, VA June 17, '64 of wounds rec. in action
Frank, William	Private	10/14/64	Substitute - Disc. July 13, '65
Freeman, Spencer	Private	08/25/63	Drafted -- Absent, sick at must. out

Name	*Rank*	*Muster In*	*Remarks*
Fry, Adam	Private	10/28/61	Killed at Pocotaligo Oct. 22, '62
Fry, Levi	Private	10/28/61	Killed at Ft. Wagner July 11, '63
Gaines, George	Private	08/26/63	Drafted -- Died July 11, '64
Giboney, George W.	Private	11/16/61	Must. out Nov. 28, '64
Gilhouse, Albert	Private	09/18/61	Deserted Oct. 20, '61
Gillen, James	Private	10/28/61	Must. out Nov. 28, '64
Gobles, William	Private	08/27/63	Drafted -- Died at Hampton, VA July 20, '64
Gray, John	Private	02/18/65	Substitute -- Must. out July 18, '65
Gray, Milton	Private	10/28/61	Must. out Nov. 28, '64
Gray, Silas	Private	10/28/61	Disc. Sept. 4, '62
Grossenbecker, Jno	Private	02/21/65	Substitute -- Must. out July 18, '65
Grossman, Frederick	Private	02/23/65	Substitute -- Must. out July 18, '65
Hagerty, Joseph	Private	01/01/64	Killed in action July 9, '64 -- Bur. near Ft. Stedman, Petersburg, VA
Hawksworth, George	Private		Not in Bates
Hawley, Isaac	Private	08/26/63	Drafted -- Absent, sick at must. out
Hempfield, George	Private	04/24/62	Trans. to Vet. Reserve Corps. Dec. 8, '63
Hench, Frederick	Private	10/28/61	Died at Hilton Head Oct. 31, '62
Henney, Levi	Private	08/27/63	Drafted -- Disc. June 2, '65
Holeman, Edward	Private	02/22/65	Substitute -- Died at Raleigh, NC June 19, '65
Hopper, Nicholas	Private	02/16/65	Substitute -- Must. out July 18, '65
Houseman, Andrew	Private	10/28/61	Trans. to Signal Corps. Oct. 16, '63
Hubbard, Michael	Private	08/26/63	Drafted -- Disc. Surgeon Certif. Apr. 24, '65
Hultz, Nathan	Private	08/27/63	Drafted -- Disc. June 9, '65
Hurley, John	Private	10/28/61	Died at Ft. Monroe Nov. 30, '61
Irwin, Jacob	Private	10/28/61	Must. out Nov. 28, '64
Jennings, Michael	Private	10/28/61	Must. out Nov. 28, '64
Johnson, John	Private	09/20/61	Deserted Oct., '61
Kelley, Atkinson	Private	08/27/63	Drafted -- Absent, sick at must. out
Kelley, Randall W.	Private	09/23/64	Drafted -- Disc. June 28, '65
Kemp, Joseph	Private	11/06/61	Died at Hilton Head July 3, '62
Kerns, Thomas	Private	02/22/65	Substitute -- Must. out July 18, '65
Kimball, Festus A.	Private	02/10/65	Substitute -- Disc. July 14, '65
Kinsel, Jonathan	Private	10/28/61	Killed at Ft. Wagner July 11, '63
Knox, William T.	Private	03/24/62	Died at Hilton Head July 28, '62
Kough, John S.	Private	10/28/61	Must. out Nov. 28, '64
Kounsman, David	Private	10/28/61	Killed at Ft. Wagner July 11, '63
Hempfield, George	Private	04/24/62	Trans. to Vet. Reserve Corps. Dec. 8, '63
Hench, Frederick	Private	10/28/61	Died at Hilton Head Oct. 31, '62
Henney, Levi	Private	08/27/63	Drafted -- Disc. June 2, '65
Holeman, Edward	Private	02/22/65	Substitute -- Died at Raleigh, NC June 19, '65
Hopper, Nicholas	Private	02/16/65	Substitute -- Must. out July 18, '65
Houseman, Andrew	Private	10/28/61	Trans. to Signal Corps. Oct. 16, '63

Name	Rank	Muster In	Remarks
Hubbard, Michael	Private	08/26/63	Drafted -- Disc. Surgeon Certif. Apr. 24, '65
Hultz, Nathan	Private	08/27/63	Drafted -- Disc. June 9, '65
Kounsman, Samuel	Private	03/24/62	Killed at Ft. Wagner July 11, '63
Krotzen, John	Private	10/28/61	Disc. Surgeon Certif. Apr. 19, '62
Krotzer, Henry	Private	10/28/61	Died at Salisbury Nov. 22, '64
Lafferty, George	Private	10/28/61	Must. out Nov. 28, '64
Langdon, John G.	Private	09/12/61	Deserted Sept. 27, '61
Laughlin, George W.	Private	02/17/65	Substitute -- Must. out July 18, '65
Leffler, William	Private	09/23/64	Drafted -- Disc. June 28, '65
Logan, James A.	Private	11/10/61	Deserted Nov. 11, '61
Martin, Andrew	Private	02/25/64	Must. out July 18, '65
Martin, Edward	Private	02/29/64	Disc. Aug. 16, '65
Matthews, Edward B.	Private	10/28/61	Disc. Surgeon Certif., date unknown
McAninch, William A.	Private	02/27/64	Must. out July 18, '65
McKeefer, Arthur	Private	07/11/63	Drafted -- Disc. Surgeon Certif. Apr. 8, '65
McKnell, Albert	Private	02/22/65	Substitute -- Must. out July 18, '65
Meadville, Graham	Private	10/28/61	Prisoner from July 13, '63 to Nov. 21, '64 -- Must. out Mar. 7, '65 to date Nov. 26, '64
Meadville, Peter	Private	10/28/61	Disc. July 15, '63
Milligan, John	Private	02/24/65	Substitute -- Must. out July 18, '65
Miller, Edmond	Private	10/18/64	Substitute -- Must. out July 18, '65
Miller, George W.	Private	10/28/61	Disc. Surgeon Certif., date unknown
Miller, James	Private	09/26/64	Drafted -- Disc. June 28, '65
Monroe, Joseph	Private	09/23/64	Drafted -- Disc. May 29, '65
Moorehouse, Samuel	Private	02/24/65	Substitute -- Must. out July 18, '65
Moorland, John	Private	10/28/61	Disc. June 23, '63
Morgan, John R.	Private	10/28/61	Killed at Ft. Wagner July 11, '63
Mumford, Alonzo O.	Private	09/28/64	Drafted -- Disc. June 28, '65
Murray, Henry	Private	02/24/65	Substitute - Disc. June 10, '65
Noles, Michael	Private	02/16/65	Substitute -- Must. out July 18, '65
Osler, John	Private	07/16/63	Drafted -- Disc. June 9, '65
Oxworth, George	Private	10/28/61	Trans. To Signal Corps. Oct. 13, '63
Powell, John	Private	02/24/64	Died at Hampton, VA Aug. 28, '64 of wounds rec. in action
Ragan, Daniel	Private	10/28/61	Died at Hilton Head July 11, '62
Ray, John M.	Private	09/23/64	Drafted -- Must. out July 18, '65
Reed, Thomas	Private	08/26/63	Drafted -- Disc. Surgeon Certif. May 8, '65
Reed, William H.	Private	10/20/64	Substitute -- Must. out July 18, '65
Rogers, Samuel F.	Private	01/25/65	Trans. from 203 PA Vol. June 22, '65 - Must. out July 18, '65
Rolles, Clement	Private	08/25/63	Drafted -- Deserted Nov. 30, '64
Rumbaugh, James	Private	07/13/63	Drafted -- Disc. May 22, '65
Shall, John	Private	08/11/64	Drafted -- Died at Wilmington, NC

Name	Rank	Muster In	Remarks
Shannon, John	Private	11/06/61	Apr. 24, '64 Disc. Aug. 1, '62
Shultz, Dallas	Private	12/28/63	Trans. to Vet. Reserve Corps. Sept. 16, '64 -- Disc. July 31, '65
Shultz, Joseph	Private	08/27/63	Drafted -- Disc. June 2, '65
Silbo, John	Private	02/21/65	Substitute -- Must. out July 18, '65
Sipe, Levi	Private	10/28/61	Died Mar. 25, '64 -- Bur. Prospect Hill Cem., York, PA
Skipper, August R.	Private	02/24/65	Substitute -- Must. out July 18, '65
Smith, George	Private	10/28/61	Disc. Feb. 28, '63
Smith, Marion	Private	10/28/61	Must. out Nov. 28, '64
Smith, Stanford	Private	10/28/61	Must. out Nov. 28, '64
Smith, William	Private	09/30/63	Drafted -- Killed at Drewy's Bluff May 14, '64
Smurr, Reason	Private	07/16/63	Drafted -- Must. out July 18, '65
Spicer, Charles	Private	10/10/64	Substitute -- Must. out July 18, '65
Stamosky, Henry	Private	02/25/65	Substitute -- Must. out July 18, '65
Steiner, Benjamin	Private	10/28/61	Killed at Pocotaligo Oct. 22, '62
Stole, Henry	Private	08/18/64	Substitute - Trans. to 203 PA Vol. June 22, '65 -- Absent, sick at must. out
Strawinger, John	Private	02/13/65	Substitute - Must. out July 18, '65
Taylor, Gilbert	Private	02/21/65	Substitute - Disc. July 7, '65
Thompson, George	Private	02/16/65	Substitute - Disc. July 18, '65
Tierney, Thomas	Private	02/27/64	Must. out July 18, '65
Vanorden, Norman G.	Private	10/24/64	Drafted -- Died at Ft. Monroe Dec. 12, '64
Weeks, Carodan	Private	08/27/63	Drafted -- Died at Andersonville Oct. 2, '64; Grave 10,217 or 10,273
Weirbaugh, Henry	Private	03/30/62	Died at Portsmouth Grove, RI Oct. 18, '64 -- Bur. record Oct. 30, '64
Weirbaugh, Levi	Private	02/24/62	Must. out May 15, '65
Welsh, David	Private	02/23/65	Substitute -- Must. out July 18, '65
Whitman, Thomas	Private	02/14/65	Substitute -- Must out July 18, '65
Wicker, Frederick	Private	10/28/61	Must. out Nov. 28, '64
Wilcox, David E.	Private	09/23/64	Drafted -- Disc. June 10, '65
Wise, John	Private	08/27/63	Drafted -- Absent, sick at must. out
Young, John	Private	01/01/64	Disc. date unknown

CRITICAL CONVERSATIONS

VOLUME 2

MOVING FROM MONOLOGUE TO DIALOGUE

NLN
National League
for Nursing

CRITICAL CONVERSATIONS

VOLUME 2

MOVING FROM MONOLOGUE TO DIALOGUE

Susan Gross Forneris, PhD, RN, CNE, CHSE-A, FAAN
Mary Fey, PhD, RN, CHSE-A, FAAN, ANEF

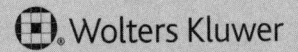

Wolters Kluwer

Philadelphia • Baltimore • New York • London
Buenos Aires • Hong Kong • Sydney • Tokyo

Vice President, Nursing Segment: Julie K. Stegman
Manager, Nursing Education and Practice Content: Jamie Blum
Senior Development Editor: Meredith L. Brittain
Marketing Manager: Brittany Clements
Editorial Assistant: Molly Kennedy
Design Coordinator: Steve Druding
Production Project Manager: Kim Cox
Manufacturing Coordinator: Karin Duffield
Prepress Vendor: Aptara, Inc.

Copyright © 2021 National League for Nursing.

Forneris, S. G., & Fey, M. (2021). *Critical Conversations, Volume 2: Moving From Monologue to Dialogue.* Washington, DC: National League for Nursing.

All rights reserved. This book is protected by copyright. No part of this book may be reproduced or transmitted in any form or by any means, including as photocopies or scanned-in or other electronic copies, or utilized by any information storage and retrieval system without written permission from the copyright owner, except for brief quotations embodied in critical articles and reviews. Materials appearing in this book prepared by individuals as part of their official duties as U.S. government employees are not covered by the above-mentioned copyright. To request permission, please contact Wolters Kluwer at Two Commerce Square, 2001 Market Street, Philadelphia, PA 19103, via email at permissions@lww.com, or via our website at shop.lww.com (products and services).

9 8 7 6 5 4 3 2 1

Printed in USA

ISBN-13: 978-1-97516-856-8

This work is provided "as is," and the publisher disclaims any and all warranties, express or implied, including any warranties as to accuracy, comprehensiveness, or currency of the content of this work.

This work is no substitute for individual patient assessment based upon healthcare professionals' examination of each patient and consideration of, among other things, age, weight, gender, current or prior medical conditions, medication history, laboratory data and other factors unique to the patient. The publisher does not provide medical advice or guidance and this work is merely a reference tool. Healthcare professionals, and not the publisher, are solely responsible for the use of this work including all medical judgments and for any resulting diagnosis and treatments.

Given continuous, rapid advances in medical science and health information, independent professional verification of medical diagnoses, indications, appropriate pharmaceutical selections and dosages, and treatment options should be made and healthcare professionals should consult a variety of sources. When prescribing medication, healthcare professionals are advised to consult the product information sheet (the manufacturer's package insert) accompanying each drug to verify, among other things, conditions of use, warnings and side effects and identify any changes in dosage schedule or contraindications, particularly if the medication to be administered is new, infrequently used or has a narrow therapeutic range. To the maximum extent permitted under applicable law, no responsibility is assumed by the publisher for any injury and/or damage to persons or property, as a matter of products liability, negligence law or otherwise, or from any reference to or use by any person of this work.

shop.lww.com   www.NLN.org

This book is dedicated to educators, who shape our thinking and encourage us always.

About the Authors

Susan Gross Forneris, PhD, RN, CNE, CHSE-A, FAAN, is currently the Director for the National League for Nursing Center for Innovation in Education Excellence, Washington, DC. Selected for inclusion in the 2010 inaugural group of NLN Simulation Leaders, she has been working in the field of simulation since 2003. She served as a simulation expert for the NLN ACE.S Team (Advancing Care Excellence for Seniors) and a simulation author for the NLN ACE.Z, Alzheimer's simulation scenario series. In her work with the NLN, she has traveled to Taiwan, China, and South Korea, working closely with those countries' nursing education influencers to further develop faculty skills in the use of simulation best practices in teaching and learning. She has been instrumental in the design and implementation of NLN faculty development courses focused on simulation pedagogy foundations, debriefing, curriculum integration, and evaluation. Dr. Forneris's expertise is in curriculum development with emphasis on debriefing in combination with her research on critical thinking. Her publications focus on the development and use of reflective teaching strategies to enhance critical thinking. She coauthored the publication *Critical Conversations: The NLN Guide for Teaching Thinking.* Susan began her nursing career with a bachelor's degree in nursing from the College of St. Scholastica, in Duluth, Minnesota. She completed both her master's and doctoral studies at the University of Minnesota in nursing education and educational psychology. Her past clinical practice includes cardiac and rehabilitation nursing, moving into medical case management for both private and insurance-based case management firms. She is a former Professor of Nursing at St. Catherine University, St. Paul, Minnesota.

About the Authors

Mary Fey, PhD, RN, CHSE-A, FAAN, ANEF, as a teacher and critical care nurse, has a keen interest in the dynamics of human interaction. Whether in a classroom, clinical area, or simulation lab, she believes that the words we choose to use and the way we choose to say them can have a profound effect on learners' motivation and their ability to take the next developmental step. It is on this teacher-learner interaction that Dr. Fey focuses her work.

Dr. Fey received her PhD from the University of Maryland, where her research focused on debriefing in simulation-based learning experiences. She is past director of the Debra L. Spunt Clinical Simulation Laboratory at the University of Maryland School of Nursing. Her work with the National League for Nursing includes coauthoring two white papers: *The NLN Vision for Teaching with Simulation* and the *NLN Vision for Debriefing Across the Curriculum*. She was recently inducted into the National League for Nursing's Academy of Nurse Educators and continues to collaborate with the NLN. She is actively involved in both the Society for Simulation in Healthcare (SSH) and the International Nursing Association for Clinical Simulation and Learning (INACSL). With the SSH, she led the development of the CHSE-A certification program. With the INACSL, she has been involved in the ongoing development of the *Standards of Best Practice: Simulation* since their inception and has served on the Board of Directors.

Dr. Fey is currently the Senior Director for Teaching and Learning at the Center for Medical Simulation; faculty in the Department of Anesthesia, Critical Care & Pain Medicine at Massachusetts General Hospital; and a lecturer at Harvard Medical School. She works with health professions faculty to improve their ability to have reflective learning conversations that hold learners to high standards while still holding them in high regard.

About the Contributor

Lisa Day, PhD, RN, CNE, FAAN, ANEF, is a Professor, Clinician Educator at the University of New Mexico College of Nursing in Albuquerque, New Mexico. Dr. Day has been involved in academic and clinical practice education since 1999 and has consulted on several national nursing education–related projects, including the Carnegie Foundation for the Advancement of Teaching's National Study of Nursing Education and the first phase of the Robert Wood Johnson Foundation–funded project Quality and Safety Education in Nursing (QSEN). She is a coauthor of the landmark publication *Educating Nurses: A Call for Radical Transformation* (Benner et al., 2010), which reports the results of the Carnegie study, and has provided many faculty development workshops and curriculum consultations for schools of nursing in the United States and Canada. She is certified as a nurse educator (CNE) by the National League for Nursing (NLN) and was selected as a Josiah Macy, Jr. Foundation Faculty Scholar in interprofessional health sciences education, 2013 to 2015. She recently coauthored with a communication scientist an innovative book on safe communication in nursing practice (Hannawa, Wendt & Day) and is currently a member of the NLN Commission for Nursing Education Accreditation (CNEA) residency program accreditation task force. In 2019, Dr. Day was inducted as a fellow in both the American Academy of Nursing and the NLN's Nurse Educator Academy.

References

Benner, P., Sutphen, M., Leonard, V., & Day, L. (2010). *Educating nurses: A call for radical transformation*. Jossey-Bass.

Hannawa, A., Wendt, A., & Day, L. (2017). New horizons in patient safety: safe communication: evidence-based core competencies with case studies from nursing practice. Walter de Gruyter GmbH & Co KG.

Prologue

In the next-generation National Council Licensure Examination (NCLEX) project, the National Council of State Boards of Nursing (NCSBN) cites the increasingly complex decisions that newly licensed nurses make during the course of patient care to support the need for new approaches to the RN licensing examination (Williams et al., 2014a; Williams et al., 2014b). The NCSBN also cites the presence of sicker patients, increasingly complex health settings, new nurses' increased stress levels, and 25% turnover of new graduate nurses to support the need for extended entry to practice programs for new nurses (National Council of State Boards of Nursing, 2020). In a report of findings and recommendations from the Carnegie national study of nursing education, Benner et al. (2010) identified the increasingly complex foundational knowledge and skills needed for new nurses to practice safely and effectively and called for a "radical transformation" in nursing education that will include an integration of classroom and clinical learning (Benner et al., 2010).

In response to these calls for transformation, nurse educators are seeking new approaches to classroom teaching and learning. Recent efforts to change nursing education, practice, and regulation emphasize the fact that new nurses preparing to confront the complexities of practice need more than to acquire knowledge as decontextualized facts and assertions provided in a lecture. New nurses' success depends on their ability to develop a sense of salience and to use the knowledge and skills that they acquire as they think and problem solve within whole clinical situations that are always underdetermined and always changing. To bring the complexities of practice to the classroom, nurse educators have started using stories, case studies, and clinical narratives in new ways. To bring authentic practice to the classroom requires that teachers and learners move from lectures to dialogues embedded in a clinical context and from questions and answers to conversations that take into account the interconnected wholeness of each clinical situation. These important efforts to transform nursing education are supported by *Critical Conversations: The NLN Guide for Teaching Thinking* (Forneris & Fey, 2018) and are extended in this second volume. These two monographs provide nurse educators with necessary tools to transform and develop their teaching in just these ways.

The value of this second volume in the NLN's *Critical Conversations* series is in the specific guidance it offers to nurse educators. Based on evidence from learning science, constructivist and experiential learning theories (Dewey, 1938; Moll, 1990), and the science and philosophy of situated cognition (Lave, 1991; Robbins & Aydede, 2009), the authors use examples and offer specific instructions to assist nurse educators in all settings to develop the skills they need to transform their teaching and maximize learning. These include skills to engage learners with spontaneous, problem-solving questions and discussions that are reflective and grounded in whole clinical encounters. This second volume continues and expands the work of the first volume by providing more in-depth theoretical background as well as specific directions for nurse educators on how to engage students in each step of the "three Cs" structure outlined in Volume

1—Context, Content, and Course—using guided questions, dialogue, and conversation to coach students in higher reasoning and knowledge-use skills.

The failure of content-driven lecture in nursing education is well known. Preparing student nurses for practice requires classroom, clinical, and lab-based learning experiences that challenge students to use knowledge to think and problem solve while they are involved in complex clinical contexts. The two volumes in the NLN's *Critical Conversations* series are tools to guide nurse educators in this transformation.

Lisa Day, PhD, RN, CNE, FAAN, ANEF
Professor, Clinician Educator
University of New Mexico College of Nursing

References

Benner, P., Sutphen, M., Leonard, V., & Day, L. (2010). *Educating nurses: A call for radical transformation*. Jossey-Bass.

Dewey, J. (1938). *Experience and education*. Macmillan.

Forneris, M. G., & Fey, M. (2018). *Critical conversations: The NLN guide for teaching thinking* (Vol. 1). Wolters Kluwer.

Lave, J. (1991). *Situated learning: Legitimate peripheral participation*. Cambridge University Press.

Moll, L. C. (1990). *Vygotsky and education: Instructional implications and applications of sociohistorical psychology*. Cambridge University Press.

National Council of State Boards of Nursing. (2020). Transition to practice: Why transition to practice (TTP)? Retrieved from https://ncsbn.org/transition-to-practice.htm

Robbins, P., & Aydede, M. (2009). *The Cambridge handbook of situated cognition*. Cambridge University Press.

Williams, N., Doyoung, K., Dickison, P., & Woo, A. (2014a). NCLEX and entry-level nurse characteristics. *Journal of Nursing Regulation, 5*, 45–49.

Williams, N., Kim, D., & Dickison, P. (2014b). Validating the NCLEX-RN test plan: Comparing practice analysis data. *Journal of Nursing Regulation, 5*, 39–43.

Contents

About the Authors vi

About the Contributor viii

Prologue ix

CHAPTER 1 **Introduction: Moving from Monologue to Dialogue** 1

CHAPTER 2 **Context** 7

CHAPTER 3 **Content** 15

CHAPTER 4 **Course** 25

Epilogue 33

List of Figures and Tables

LIST OF FIGURES

Figure 1.1   Cognitive architecture and learning sequence 3
Figure 3.1   Illustration of designing instruction: chunking 17
Figure 3.2   Illustration of designing instruction: interleaving 21

LIST OF TABLES

Table 1.1   Educator Communication Examples 2
Table 2.1   Designing Instruction: Creating the Context for Learning 11
Table 3.1   Designing Instruction: Chunking 18
Table 3.2   Designing Instruction: Schema 19
Table 3.3   Designing Instruction: Interleaving 22
Table 4.1   Example of Critical Reflection Dialogue Technique 26
Table 4.2   Designing Instruction: Collaborative Cognition 29
Table 4.3   Designing Instruction: Analogical Transfer 30

Introduction: Moving from Monologue to Dialogue

John Dewey, one the most prominent figures in educational reform, believed that education should prepare individuals to understand the nature of the world in which they live through the development of their capacity to think critically. He believed that this preparation included opportunities for discussion, applying experiences and ideas, seeing problems, relating facts, and enjoying ideas (Alexander, 1987; Dewey, 1933, 1958). Dewey believed that learners learn best through immersive experiences in which inquiry and perspective taking happen naturally. Look at the image above. As you began this chapter, you may have thought, "What is this image about? What does this image have to do with what I am reading?" Nonetheless, it was the beginning of an internal monologue with yourself—a way to begin to make sense of something. The early Greek philosophers differentiated human beings from other species by our ability to use language. Especially in education, the correct use of language—providing direction, being informative, expressing ideas, and asking questions—is most effective when learners are engaged in a discourse of *meaning making*. Once upon a time, professors actually shared their knowledge through the language of story without using PowerPoint, overhead projectors, or even chalkboards. Storytelling is one of the oldest means of communication and exists in every culture. The use of story or narrative in nursing helps learners embrace nursing values and experiences that are important, unique, and

TABLE 1.1

Educator Communication Examples

Educator Dialogue	Strategy/Purpose
EXAMPLE #1 In your prep for class, you read about priorities for consideration for our vulnerable aging adults who are managing fluid balance issues. Let's review those priorities: *educator lists the priorities*	Teaching content

EXAMPLE #2
In your prep for class, you read about priorities for consideration for our vulnerable aging adults who are managing fluid balance issues.
Let's examine some patient scenarios. Consider the following patients:
  1. Age: 1 year old; severe gastroenteritis
  2. Age: 60 years old; severe gastroenteritis
Walk me through your thinking on how age, in these two cases, impacts your nursing assessment and priorities for care when managing fluid balance disturbances.
	Teaching the learner to *use* the content

meaningful (Fitzpatrick, 2018). The key to effective use of story in nursing education is the ability to use a story that creates dialogue—a two-way conversation that generates related stories, questions, perspectives, and thinking. Stories are a natural link to dialogue. The storyboard at the beginning of this chapter may have evoked some thoughts and ideas, questions and answers, feelings and emotions. Yet, while this can be interpreted as a dialogue in our head, it is in reality a one-sided dialogue—or a monologue. Without the opportunity to link story with dialogue, perspectives can be missed or misinterpreted. Story may engage the mind. The ability to engage the mind using dialogue *to make meaning* lies at the heart of what Dewey would identify as great education. Great educators move beyond the monologue; instead of teaching content, they collaborate with learners, helping them think about how to use the content.

Consider the examples in Table 1.1. In contrast to Example #1, which is a monologue by the educator, it is clear that Example #2 lays the foundation for a story, opening up a dialogue to assist learners to begin to explore and understand the salient features of this story, raise awareness of any biases or assumptions, and see subtle cues to activate their knowledge. The educator is engaging the learners to begin *using the content* for which they prepared. This strategy positions the learners to better achieve an understanding of the new content.

The ultimate goal of dialogue is to achieve understanding. Schon's (1983, 1987) seminal work posits that learners must be coached and mentored through a reflective dialogue to operationalize a thinking process so that one can begin to make connections between the means and methods employed and the results achieved. Dialogue includes the back talk and mental interactivity that we engage in to further examine the influence of context and make the appropriate connections and associations between fact, concepts, rules, and principles. Through dialogue, a complete understanding of the situation is shaped. Dialogue becomes reflective as the "'situation talks back', when one responds to the 'back-talk'" (Schon, 1983, p. 79). *Critical Conversations: Moving from Monologue to Dialogue* is about using dialogue in a purposeful way. When we engage our learners in a reflective discourse, we are engaging their minds.

A VISION FOR NURSING EDUCATION

The National League for Nursing (NLN) has consistently challenged nurse educators to learn about and implement teaching methodologies that prepare our future nurses to practice in a participatory and information-driven consumer environment. Published vision statements highlight the development of resources for faculty to develop their expertise using advanced teaching techniques to support the development of high-level reasoning skills throughout a program of learning (NLN, 2015a, 2015b). In response to these recommendations, *The NLN Guide for Teaching Thinking* (Forneris & Fey, 2016) and *Critical Conversations: The NLN Guide For Teaching Thinking* (Forneris & Fey, 2018) were the first in a series of resources for faculty development to enhance teaching and learning through the use of dialogue rooted in critical theory—a foundation to engage learner thinking and reasoning. Transforming nursing education requires a reframing of the teaching-learning process so that the emphasis is focused less on *content* and more on strategies that guide students to *use the content*.

The Science and Art of Teaching and Learning

Building faculty expertise in the teaching of higher-level reasoning skills is paramount for future generations of learners. As educators, we often believe in the misconception that learners are empty vessels into which content can be poured. Content, in and of itself, compelling as it may seem, cannot teach itself. Recent advances in neuroscience research are unveiling intriguing discoveries about how our brain functions and, more importantly, how brain-based learning is changing the face of education today (Alexander et al., 2019; Argawal, 2019; Cardoza, 2011; Doyle & Zakrajsek, 2019; Pan & Rickard, 2018; Weidman & Baker, 2015).

Learning in its simplest form requires an understanding of the learning sequence whereby a learner first attends to outside information in sensory memory. Once attended to, the brain transfers information from short-term memory (where it is consciously processed) to long-term memory (where it is stored and then retrieved when needed later) (Deans for Impact, 2015); see also Figure 1.1. The key is to focus on the teaching and

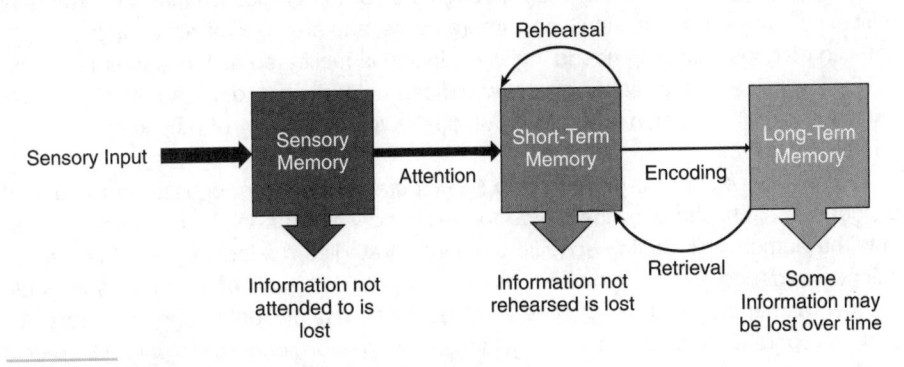

FIGURE 1.1 Cognitive architecture and learning sequence.

learning strategies that help learners to consciously process information in short-term memory so that the information is properly encoded for later use.

Learners' ability to understand new ideas may be impaired if they are confronted with too much information all at once (Deans for Impact, 2015). Neuroscience research is now telling us more about how the brain works as it is learning. The outputs of these studies communicate that many once tested-and-proven strategies do not appear to be as effective with today's learners. Today's learners are characterized as being technology consumers—often described as digital natives or learners who crave digital solutions. While they are known to struggle with attention, they desire practical, relevant, immediate, and visually engaging learning opportunities while being as technologically advanced as possible. This new research on teaching and learning can be used as a guide for educators in their work as they engage today's learners (Argawal, 2019; Bae et al., 2019; Birnbaum et al., 2013; Bjork et al., 2015; Brown et al., 2014; Bui & McDaniel, 2015; Martin et al., 2016). Cognitive principles that stand firm include (1) the ability for learners to think about and pay attention to meaning and (2) the importance of the nature of deliberate practice in the learning of new information (Deans for Impact, 2016). *Critical Conversations: Moving from Monologue to Dialogue* will take a deeper dive into the neuroscience of teaching and learning, linking the *Guide* with contemporary strategies rooted in today's neuroscience.

Linking Dialogue with Content

Critical Conversations: The NLN Guide for Teaching Thinking (Forneris & Fey, 2018) provided a foundation by offering practical guidance for the learning conversations that are at the heart of understanding the sense-making that learners engage in. This first monograph identified *high leverage points* in educator/learner interactions—moments when we partner with learners, using perspectives, to cocreate meaning. We explored the *NLN Guide for Teaching Thinking* (National League for Nursing, 2017) across the phases of Context, Content, and Course. We provided a framework for the educator to explore how the learner makes sense of information and guide thinking in each of these phases of the conversation. Context provides the place for reflection to begin—the situation or concept being explored (Dreifuerst, 2009; Forneris & Fey, 2016). Reflection is used to guide the learner to uncover areas for consideration. The subsequent exploration centers on how Content is used and understood through the veil of perspective that is informed by past experiences, current knowledge, impressions, and so on, all of which help the educator to diagnose learning needs. Finally, thinking is facilitated as the learner is guided to discern key aspects that form a new conceptual understanding. A new Course for understanding and action emerges to guide the learner in use of new knowledge for future action.

Critical Conversations: Moving from Monologue to Dialogue focuses on the use of dialogue in each phase of the *Guide for Teaching Thinking*. In the chapters that follow, the authors will outline specific teaching strategies guided by the latest neuroscience evidence and how they are used and applied in each of the phases to guide teacher-learner interactions. Chapter 2 will guide the use of Context through strategies that incorporate psychological safety, situated cognition, and scaffolding. Chapter 3 provides direct links to guiding learners to use their Content through brain science strategies that incorporate elements of time, cognitive load, and retrieval practices. Finally, Chapter 4 focuses on guiding learners to rehearse their knowledge, setting a Course for the transfer of new learning to a future course of action.

References

Alexander, T. M. (1987). *John Dewey's theory of art, experience, and nature: The horizons of feeling*. State University of New York Press.

Alexander, B., Ashford-Rowe, K., Barajas-Murph, N., Dobbin, G., Knott, J., McCormack, M., Pomerantz, J., Seilhamer, R. & Weber, N. (2019). *Horizon Report 2019 Higher Education Edition*. EDU19. Retrieved from https://www.learntechlib.org/p/208644

Argawal, P. K. (2019). Retrieval practice and Bloom's Taxonomy: Do students need fact knowledge before higher order learning? *Journal of Educational Psychology, 111*(2), 189–209. https://doi.org/10.1037/edu0000282

Bae, C. L., Therriault, D. J., & Redifer, J. L. (2019). Investigating the testing effect: Retrieval as a characteristic of effective study strategies. *Learning and Instruction, 60,* 206–214. https://doi.org/10.1016/j.learninstruc.2017.12.008

Birnbaum, M. S., Kornell, N., Bjork, E. L., & Bjork, R. A. (2013). Why interleaving enhances inductive learning: The roles of discrimination and retrieval. *Memory and Cognition, 41*(3), 392–402. https://doi.org/10.3758/s13421-012-0272-7

Bjork, E. L., Soderstrom, N. C., & Little, J. L. (2015). Can multiple-choice testing induce desirable difficulties? Evidence from the laboratory and the classroom. *The American Journal of Psychology, 128*(2), 229–239. https://www.jstor.org/stable/10.5406/amerjpsyc.128.2.0229

Brown, P. C., Roediger III, H. L., & McDaniel, M. A. (2014). *Make it stick: The science of successful learning*. Belknap Press.

Bui, D. C., & McDaniel, M. A. (2015). Enhancing learning during lecture note-taking using outlines and illustrative diagrams. *Journal of Applied Research in Memory and Cognition, 4*(2), 129–135. https://doi.org/10.1016/j.jarmac.2015.03.002

Cardoza, M. P. (2011). Neuroscience and simulation: An evolving theory of brain-based education. *Clinical Simulation in Nursing, 7*(6), e205–e208. https://doi.org/10.1016/j.ecns.2011.08.004

Deans for Impact. (2015). *The Science of Learning*. Retrieved from https://deansforimpact.org/resources/the-science-of-learning

Deans for Impact. (2016). *Practice with Purpose: The Emerging Science of Teacher Expertise*. Retrieved from https://deansforimpact.org/resources/practice-with-purpose

Dewey, J. (1933). *How we think: A restatement of the relation of reflective thinking to the educative process* (2nd ed.). Heath and Company.

Dewey, J. (1958). *Philosophy of education*. Littlefield, Adams and Co.

Doyle, T., & Zakrajsek, T. (2019). *The new science of learning: How to learn in harmony with your brain* (2nd ed.). Stylus Publishing.

Dreifuerst, K. T. (2009). The essentials of debriefing in simulation learning: a concept analysis. *Nursing Education Perspectives, 30*(2), 109–114.

Fitzpatrick, J. J. (2018). Teaching through storytelling: Narrative nursing. *Nursing Education Perspectives, 39*(2), 60. https://doi.org/10.1097/01.NEP.0000000000000298

Forneris, S. G., & Fey, M. (2016). Critical conversations: The NLN guide to teaching thinking. *Nursing Education Perspectives, 37*(5), 248–249. https://doi.org/10.1097/01.NEP.0000000000000069

Forneris, S. G., & Fey, M. (Eds.) (2018). *Critical conversations: The NLN guide for teaching thinking*. National League for Nursing.

Martin, N. D., Nguyen, K., & McDaniel, M. A. (2016). Structure building differences influence learning from educational text: Effects on encoding, retention, and metacognitive control. *Contemporary Educational*

Psychology, 46, 52–60. https://doi.org/10.1016/j.cedpsych.2016.03.005

National League for Nursing. (2015a). *A vision for teaching with simulation*. Retrieved from http://www.nln.org/docs/default-source/about/nln-vision-series-(position-statements)/vision-statement-a-vision-for-teaching-with-simulation.pdf?sfvrsn=2

National League for Nursing. (2015b). *Debriefing across the curriculum*. Retrieved from http://www.nln.org/docs/default-source/about/nln-vision-series-(position-statements)/nln-vision-debriefing-across-the-curriculum.pdf?sfvrsn=0

National League for Nursing. (2017). *Critical conversations: The NLN guide for teaching thinking*. Retrieved from http://www.nln.org/docs/default-source/professional-development-programs/nln-guide-to-teaching-thinking.pdf?sfvrsn=2

Pan, S. C., & Rickard, T. C. (2018). Transfer of test-enhanced learning: Meta-analytic review and synthesis. *Psychological Bulletin, 144*(7), 710–756. https://doi.org/10.1037/bul0000151

Schon, D. (1983). *The reflective practitioner*. Basic Books, Inc.

Schon, D. (1987). *Educating the reflective practitioner*. Jossey-Bass, Inc.

Weidman, J. & Baker, K. (2015). The cognitive science of learning: Concepts and strategies for the educator and learner. *Neuroscience in Anesthesiology and Perioperative Medicine, 121*(6), 1586–1599. https://doi.org/10.1213/ANE.0000000000000890

2

Context

Context, within the 3C framework (Context, Content, and Course), has two meanings. The first involves the environment for learning that is created by the educator. The second meaning is the contextual factors that influence nursing care decisions. This chapter will explore each in turn.

A DIALOGUE

Creating a Context for learning—that is, the learning environment—sets the stage for the experience and involves consideration of educator, learner, and environmental factors that influence the situation. Research on the neuroscience of learning has provided educators with evidence that can guide the creation of an optimal learning environment (Cozolino & Sprokay, 2006; Dweck, 2016; Edmondson, 2019; Lerner et al., 2015; Okon-Singer et al., 2015; Rudolph et al., 2014). This same research also supports long-held theoretical beliefs about learning: that experience, coupled with feedback and reflection, is a powerful way to learn; and that as social learners, dialogue is a powerful teaching/learning strategy. This dialogue, a type of critical conversation, is a purposeful learning conversation, with structure, process, and outcome goals. These critical conversations explore learners' perspectives and thought processes, provide feedback on performance and thinking, and chart a course for the next stage of development. The overall goal within the context of educating health professions students is the development of skilled practitioners with the ability to self-monitor their own practice. These critical conversations have been shown to be the most powerful strategy for learning and achievement (Johnson et al., 2016).

Perhaps the most influential factor in the learning environment is the educator's view of the teacher-learner interaction with regard to the errors and missteps that are a welcome and inevitable part of learning. Many of the active learning strategies discussed in this book will be challenging to learners: retrieval practice, interleaving, and analogical transfer, to name a few. At times, learning in this way can seem slower and appear to take more effort than simply memorizing, testing, and moving on. It is true that these strategies require more effort and may be perceived as "difficult." This effort has the desirable outcome, however, of creating durable, flexible learning—hence, the term "desirable difficulties" (Yan et al., 2016). As our learners engage in these desirable difficulties, errors made in the process of learning should be used as powerful triggers for reflective learning.

Frequently, when an educator encounters a student error, the first impulse is to focus on and fix the action. This strategy may work well for some situations, such as teaching simple psychomotor tasks, but it is not sufficient to guide learners in complex, multifaceted situations. In complex situations, learners must first come to understand the nuances and complexities before the meaning is understood or action can be taken. Seeing the learners as meaning-makers, rather than simply as doers of correct or incorrect actions, then shifts the role of the educator (National League for Nursing, 2015). This shift involves the educators seeing themselves not just as transmitters of information and judges of correct or incorrect actions but as cognitive detectives, seeking to understand how learners are making sense of a situation. This shifts the focus of teaching activities from simple correction to a curious and respectful conversation aimed at understanding the learners' unique perspectives. The educator's view of learners' error and the response to it can aid or impede learning, as learners quickly adapt to the educator's response. An educator response that helps the learner examine the thought behind the observable action with curiosity and respect is likely to lead to motivation to learn and improve. When learners are met with shame or humiliation by the educator, they are more likely to instead exhibit defensiveness and/or withdrawal, with a desire to hide errors (Bynum & Artino, 2018; Dweck, 2016). An approach that seeks to understand the learner's thinking begins with dialogue. Only through dialogue can an educator understand how the learner was making sense of a situation, and why that learner took that course of action. It is through examination of the learner's thought processes, knowledge base, assumptions, and biases that educators can accurately diagnose learning needs. Once these learning needs are identified, the educator can guide the learner in generating new ways of seeing and acting in a situation (Marshak, 2019).

Learners bring all of their past experiences, culture, learning, ideas, assumptions, rules, and principles to each learning encounter, shaping how they construct knowledge (Forneris and Fey, 2016). Importantly, learners see the current situation through the filter of those past experiences, with all of the biases and assumptions built up over time. These filters can have a profound influence on how a learner makes sense of a situation from the start and impact many steps along the way. These filters affect what the learner selects to pay attention to, how the learner interprets incoming data, and how the learner prioritizes actions when forming a judgment and taking action.

Environmental factors to consider include the learning objectives, available resources, guidelines regarding confidentiality, and level of learner evaluation. Learning objectives that are clear, measurable, and developmentally appropriate should serve as a guide to learners and form the basis for the assessment of the learner. The level of assessment for the experience should be clear to learners so that they understand whether their performance (e.g., participation in class, classroom assessment activities, low-stakes quizzes, unit exams, skills testing, simulation and clinical activities, and so on) will in any way affect their grade. Formative assessment, done for the purpose of learning, is not graded and has different expectations and rules than a summative evaluation, which will be graded and may affect the learners' ability to progress in their program of study (Dixon & Worrell, 2016; Rudolph et al., 2014).

PSYCHOLOGICAL SAFETY

Creating a context in which learners can feel safe to share their thinking, admit when they do not know something, and can be receptive to feedback requires specific approaches and actions on the part of the educator. Creating this context requires attention to the whole learner—both cognition and emotion. Recent research in neuropsychology and neuroscience points to the primacy of emotion in decision-making and the impact of emotion on cognitive abilities (Lerner et al., 2015; Okon-Singer et al., 2015; Pessoa, 2015). Emotional activation brought about by the challenge of the learning situation is a double-edged sword: too little and learners are not engaged, too much and the ability to make decisions is impaired. Emotions such as stress and anxiety can profoundly impact selective attention, executive control, and working memory (Okon-Singer et al., 2015). In fact, a learning environment in which negative emotions such as stress and anxiety are minimized while positive emotional arousal is maintained creates conditions in which learners are better able to incorporate new information (Boud & Molloy, 2013; Carless & Boud, 2018; Cozolino & Sprokay, 2006; Henderson et al., 2019; Johnson et al., 2016). Conversely, learning environments marked by excessive stress and anxiety can have negative impacts on current learning that persist past the actual learning event, negatively impacting motivation for future learning (Jeffries, 2012; LeBlanc et al., 2015; Lerner et al., 2015).

The overall goal for the learning environment is to create one that is not free from stress but, instead, one in which learners are willing to experience some discomfort in the service of learning (Edmondson, 2019; Rudolph et al., 2014). This type of environment is referred to as a psychologically safe environment. Rudolph et al. (2014) describe this environment as one in which learners can face professionally meaningful challenges while being held to high standards, yet absent of the fear of shame or humiliation if errors are made.

There are specific steps that educators can take to create and maintain a positive learning environment in any context:

› Explicitly express respect for the learners as meaning-makers who are sincerely trying to do their best.

- Purposefully create a trusting teacher-learner relationship; in this environment, learners can focus on improvement, not on covering up mistakes,
- Create a learner-centered environment—one in which the focus is on exploring the learner's true learning gaps, not on the predetermined agenda of the educator.
- Embrace wrong answers, confusion, and errors as a welcome and unavoidable part of the process of learning and growth.

The environment that we create has a profound effect on learning. In an environment of trust, the educational payoff is real: learners are more willing to examine and re-order their thinking, attend to feedback, and—ultimately—to improve their practice (Rudolph et al., 2014; Sargeant et al., 2018).

The other meaning of Context in the 3C framework refers to the many factors in an episode of nursing care that affect practice decisions. These contextual factors may relate to the patient, setting, and care provider. Patient factors may include the acuity of the illness, age, socioeconomic status, and ability to participate in care decisions. Contextual factors in the care setting may include available resources, composition of the health care team, and type of facility. Who is providing the care is a factor with regard to the skill level of the provider, the provider's philosophical beliefs, and values related to health care. These individual factors and/or the interactions among them influence how care is provided. Consideration of these multiple factors is aligned with the theory of situated cognition, introduced by Lave and Wenger in their seminal work (1991). They posit that cognition does not take place entirely in the mind of the agent but rather is a result of the interaction of internal and external factors. Situated cognition theorists hypothesize that intelligent behavior arises from the interaction between the subject and the subject's environment. Distinct from information processing models—which see the mind more like a computer that takes in, processes, and stores information—the situated cognition model posits that information and knowledge do not exist prior to the interaction but that information and knowledge emerge from that interaction (Roth & Jornet, 2013). In the same way, there are factors internal to the learner that will affect how the learner makes meaning in each situation. What might be the internal factors influencing the learner? Past experience and knowledge that causes the learner to frame the situation a particular way; biases that favor a certain course of action; values and cultural beliefs that may affect what the learner attends to. Seeing learning as context dependent in this way is particularly suited to nursing practice, in which patient care situations are often complex and ill defined. Before decision-making or action is initiated, the (student) nurse must take multiple factors into account.

TEACHING AND LEARNING STRATEGIES FOR CREATING A CONTEXT FOR LEARNING

Strategies that educators can use to create a context for learning are framing the situation, norming the educational experience, and activating prior knowledge. These techniques allow learners to orient themselves, set expectations, and build on previous learning.

Framing is a teaching strategy in which the educator explicitly provides an overview of the learning experience. Learners are much more likely to actively engage in learning

TABLE 2.1

Designing Instruction: Creating the Context for Learning

Topic: Family Presence During Resuscitation

Educator Dialogue	Strategy/Purpose
We are going to spend time today discussing the pros and cons of having families present during resuscitation efforts. This is an area that has no clear right or wrong answer—so as you work to understand the issues, you may find yourself changing your position on the issue and/or in disagreement with others in the class. Missteps and changing your mind are a normal part of the learning process—don't see this as a mistake. Rather, see it as an opportunity to learn and refine your understanding. As we debate, please assume the best of each other—that we are all intelligent people doing our best to understand a complex issue. Your role is to participate by both sharing your views and listening actively to your peers' views.	Create psychological safety
One of the things that will be important to our discussion is to understand that the solution in one situation may be different from another situation. For example, would we see this differently in a pediatric case compared to an adult? Does the behavior of the family member influence our view? It's not a one-size-fits-all situation.	Acknowledge situated cognition
Much of what we talk about will be new to you. Here's what I hope to accomplish today: • You'll realize the many complexities of this issue. • You'll develop clarity around your position and values regarding family presence at resuscitations. Your role will be to engage in discussion, bringing information from your prior reading to this conversation. My role is to facilitate the conversation, add information where necessary, and explain concepts that are unclear.	Framing
I realize that you have limited knowledge of this topic and very little real-world experience. That's right where you should be at this point in your development. Please speak up when we get to something that you need more clarity about.	Norming
Let's start by thinking about a couple of issues: 1. Families as a source of support to patients 2. Complexity of teamwork and task work involved in resuscitations. Let's start with family involvement in care. What do you recall about this?	Activate prior knowledge

when they understand the learning objectives, what is expected of them, and what they can expect from the educator (Andrieux & Proteau, 2016; Clark & Fey, 2019; Rudolph et al., 2014).

Included in the overview is the strategy of norming or situating the current learning experience in the learners' developmental trajectory and providing them with information about and strategies to deal with the challenges ahead. By doing this, educators can encourage perseverance in learners as they work to master complex material.

Prior to the introduction of new information, activating prior knowledge related to the current learning experience serves two purposes: (1) repeated retrieval of previous learning is a step toward mastering the use of content knowledge; and (2) connecting the previously mastered content to the new content allows learners to see the progression of learning (Weidman & Baker, 2015). To maximize learning with this technique, educators should couple retrieval of prior knowledge with explanations of facts and elaboration of concepts (Endres et al., 2017). An example of how an educator might create the context for learning is provided in Table 2.1.

In this chapter, context has been discussed from two perspectives. Creating a safe learning environment establishes a context for learning in which learners are more likely to see connections between old and new learning, to speak up when they need help, and to incorporate feedback into practice. Context also refers to the many factors that influence care decisions. These factors can be related to the environment, the care provider, or the patient and can only be understood in terms of how they influence our knowledge of the situation.

References

Andrieux, M., & Proteau, L. (2016). Observational learning: Tell beginners what they are about to watch and they will learn better. *Frontiers in Psychology*, (7)51. https://doi.org/10.3389/fpsyg.2016.00051

Boud, D., & Molloy, E. (Eds.). (2013). *Feedback in higher and professional education: Understanding it and doing it well*. Routledge.

Bynum, W. E., & Artino Jr., A. R. (2018). Who am I, and who do I strive to be? Applying a theory of self-conscious emotions to medical education. *Academic Medicine*, 93(6), 874–880. https://doi.org/10.1097/ACM.0000000000001970

Carless, D., & Boud, D. (2018). The development of student feedback literacy: Enabling uptake of feedback. *Assessment & Evaluation in Higher Education*, 43(8), 1315–1325. https://doi.org/10.1080/02602938.2018.1463354

Clark, C., & Fey, M. (2019). Civility in learning conversations: Introducing the PAAIL communication strategy. *Nurse Educator*, 45(3), 139–143. https://doi.org/10.1097/NNE.0000000000000731

Cozolino, L., & Sprokay, S. (2006). Neuroscience and adult learning. *The Neuroscience of Adult Learning: New Directions for Adult and Continuing Education*, 2006(110), 11. https://doi.org/10.1002/ace

Dixson, D. D., & Worrell, F. C. (2016). Formative and summative assessment in the classroom. *Theory into Practice*, 55(2), 153–159. https://doi.org/10.1080/00405841.2016.1148989

Dweck, C. (2016). *Mindset: Changing the way you think to fulfil your potential* (updated ed.). Random House.

Endres, T., Carpenter, S., Martin, A., & Renkl, A. (2017). Enhancing learning by retrieval: Enriching free recall with elaborative prompting. *Learning and Instruction*, 49, 13–20. https://doi.org/10.1016/j.learninstruc.2016.11.010

Edmondson, A. C. (2019). *The fearless organization: Creating psychological safety in the workplace for learning, innovation, and growth*. Wiley.

Forneris, S. G., & Fey, M. K. (2016). Critical conversations: The NLN guide for teaching thinking. *Nursing Education Perspectives*, 37(5), 248–249. https://doi.org/10.1097/01.NEP.0000000000000069

Henderson, M., Ryan, T., & Phillips, M. (2019). The challenges of feedback in higher education. *Assessment & Evaluation in Higher Education*, 44(8), 1237–1252. https://doi.org/10.1080/02602938.2019.1599815

Jeffries, P. R. (2012). *Simulation in nursing education: From conceptualization to evaluation*. National League for Nursing.

Johnson, C. E., Keating, J. L., Boud, D. J., Dalton, M., Kiegaldie, D., Hay, M., & Palermo, C. (2016). Identifying educator behaviors for high quality verbal feedback in health professions education: Literature review and expert refinement. *BMC Medical Education, 16*(1), 96. https://doi.org/10.1186/s12909-016-0613-5

Lave, J., & Wenger, E. (1991). *Situated learning: Legitimate peripheral participation*. Cambridge University Press.

LeBlanc, V. R., McConnell, M. M., & Monteiro, S.D. (2015). Predictable chaos: A review of the effects of emotions on attention, memory and decision making. *Advances in Health Sciences Education, 20*(1), 265–282. https://doi.org/10.1007/s10459-014-9516-6

Lerner, J. S., Li, Y., Valdesolo, P., & Kassam, K. S. (2015). Emotion and decision making. *Annual Review of Psychology, 66*, 799–823. https://doi.org/10.1146/annurev-psych-010213-115043

Marshak, R. J. (2019). Dialogic Meaning-Making in Action. *Leadership and Organization and Development Review, 51(2)*, 26–51.

National League for Nursing (2015). *Debriefing across the curriculum*. Retrieved from http://www.nln.org/docs/default-source/about/nln-vision-series-(position-statements)/nln-vision-debriefing-across-the-curriculum.pdf?sfvrsn=0

Okon-Singer, H., Hendler, T., Pessoa, L., & Shackman, A. J. (2015). The neurobiology of emotion–cognition interactions: Fundamental questions and strategies for future research. *Frontiers in Human Neuroscience, 9*, 58. https://doi.org/10.3389/fnhum.2015.00058

Pessoa, L. (2015). Précis on the cognitive-emotional brain. *Behavioral and Brain Sciences, 38*, 1–66. https://doi.org/10.1017/S0140525X14000120

Roth, W. M., & Jornet, A. (2013). Situated cognition. *Wiley Interdisciplinary Reviews: Cognitive Science, 4*(5), 463–478. https://doi.org/10.1002/wcs.1242

Rudolph, J. W., Raemer, D. B., & Simon, R. (2014). Establishing a safe container for learning in simulation: The role of the presimulation briefing. *Simulation in Healthcare, 9*(6), 339–349. https://doi.org/10.1097/SIH.0000000000000047

Sargeant, J., Lockyer, J. M., Mann, K., Armson, H., Warren, A., Zetkulic, M., Soklaridis, S., Könings, K. D., Ross, K., Silver, I., & Holmboe, E. (2018). The R2C2 model in residency education: How does it foster coaching and promote feedback use? *Academic Medicine, 93*(7), 1055–1063. https://doi.org/10.1097/ACM.0000000000002131

Weidman, J., & Baker, K. (2015). The cognitive science of learning: Concepts and strategies for the educator and learner. *Anesthesia & Analgesia, 121*(6), 1586–1599. https://doi.org/10.1213/ANE.0000000000000890

Yan, V. X., Clark, C. M., & Bjork, R. A. (2016). Memory and metamemory considerations in the instruction of human beings revisited: Implications for optimizing online learning. In J. C. Horvath, J. Lodge, & J. A. C. Hattie (Eds.), *From the laboratory to the classroom: Translating the learning sciences for teachers*. Routledge.

3

Content

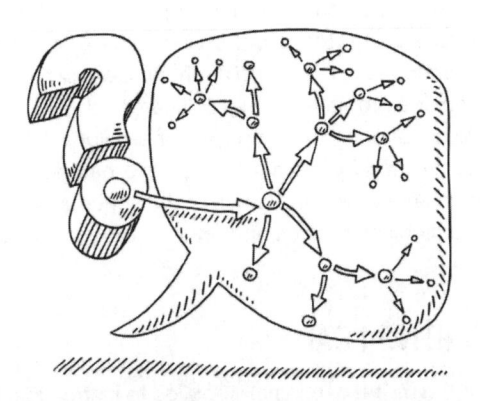

Once Context has been established, we transition teaching to understand how the learner interprets the pieces and connections of the story. Immersion into Content is a deep dive to examine learning needs and gaps and how learner knowledge, assumptions, perspective, impressions, and past experiences inform the learner's understanding (i.e., situated cognition). This process takes time, which is both static and dynamic: (1) static—the learner's past and its influence on current and future thinking; and (2) dynamic—the educator taking time and giving time to contribute to achieving content outcomes that shape future action (Forneris, 2004).

Content is defined as knowledge or information that a learner is using within the Context of a situation (Forneris & Fey, 2018). This knowledge or information is selected and used by learners based on how they interpret the context. As teachers and facilitators, we are curious to understand the what, how, and why of the pieces of knowledge that a learner has extracted. Key to an immersive process of content is the reflective dialogue; a dialogue that enables learners to share *what* they know, *how* they know, and *why* it is important. The teacher enables this content immersion through a reflective problem-posing dialogue. Curiosity is open and objective—reflecting and sharing thinking, without judgment (Argyris, 1992; Argyris & Schon, 1974; Mezirow, 1978, 1990, 2000; Schon, 1983, 1987).

An important aspect in beginning processing of content is a solid sense of learner engagement with the content. The educator as both investigator and diagnostician prepares assessment activities to determine both gaps and levels of learner understanding. This information influences the direction that the educator takes with learning strategies moving forward (e.g., managing cognitive load, amount of scaffolding, type of retrieval practice needed, and so on). These assessment strategies can be as simple as posing reflective questions, low-stakes pretests, or electronic polling with debriefing of responses during the presentation of content (Weidman & Baker, 2015).

These cognitive strategies are aimed at helping learners assimilate new knowledge as their expertise grows. A key cognitive process that is taking shape during learning encounters, one that the educator can influence, is the development of schema (plural, "schemata" or "schemas"). A schema is the general knowledge that a person possesses related to a domain. When the strands of information are connected in a meaningful way, a schema has been created—for example, what "late-stage labor" looks like, how a normally developing 2-year-old behaves (Ruiter et al., 2012). Information knit together in this way is encoded in long-term memory and can be retrieved when needed for problem recognition and problem solving. Educators play a key role in helping learners see the connections, favoring the formation of a helpful schema. As learners progress, providing opportunities for learners to retrieve past learning for application to new problems serves to strengthen and broaden the schema. Managing cognitive load, scaffolding learning, analogical transfer, and retrieval practice all support this important cognitive process.

MANAGING COGNITIVE LOAD

Cognitive load theory (Sweller, 1994), originally applied to instructional design, provides an important framework for the understanding of working memory in learning situations. Humans have two memory systems, long-term and working (i.e., short-term) memory. Long-term memory has unlimited capacity to store learned patterns and retrieve them when faced with the same or similar situations in the future. Working memory, on the other hand, processes and organizes new information. It is limited in duration and in the amount of information that it can process at any given time (Josephen, 2015; Meguerdichian et al., 2016; Van Merriënboer & Sweller, 2010).

Long-term memory is at work when we complete our usual drive to work with little concentrated effort; in fact, we can listen to music, have a conversation, or think about the upcoming day. Driving in a new city, however, is very different. We have to *concentrate*—that is, turn off the music, hang up the phone, and focus on street signs. This is because, in nonroutine situations, our working memory is activated—perceiving data, processing information, making judgments, and evaluating progress. Working memory is our ability to keep *multiple balls in the air* at the same time as we interpret data and make decisions. Similarly, in novel learning situations, students are limited in the amount of incoming data that they can pay attention to and process.

Cognitive load theory posits three types of cognitive load. Intrinsic cognitive load is determined by the complexity of the problem (e.g., performing cardiopulmonary resuscitation has low intrinsic cognitive load compared with running a resuscitation).

Extraneous cognitive load includes demands on working memory that are not relevant to the learning goals and should be minimized to the extent possible (e.g., including unimportant details in lessons). Working memory is highly susceptible to extraneous cognitive load. Germane cognitive load refers to the effort that learners make to construct schemas or mental models that can be applied to solving similar problems in the future (e.g., activating prior knowledge to help learners connect existing knowledge and skills to new situations) (Sweller, 1994).

There are several ways to thoughtfully integrate the principles of cognitive load into teacher-learner interactions. To manage the limited capacity of working memory, new information and experiences must be unfolded in a controlled way. Portioning new information in such a way that learners can process the information in a stepwise fashion is referred to as "chunking" (Chase & Simon, 1973). Chunking is a purposeful approach to designing instruction that follows several general principles:

- Teach from the simple to the complex.
- Build on existing knowledge.
- Be specific about the important elements to be learned.
- Circle back frequently to important concepts and ideas as complexity is built.
- Present a limited number of problem situations to illustrate application.
- Repeat and check in with learners along the way (Gobet, 2005).

Each subject area will have multiple chunks. The chunks can be determined by identifying elements of a subject that are closely bound to each other and grouping those elements into one chunk. Connections are then made between chunks (Figure 3.1 and Table 3.1).

Another source of extraneous cognitive load to be considered in the context of learning is emotion. Emotions modulate what we pay attention to, how we interpret data from the environment, and our ability to make judgments (LeBlanc et al., 2015; Pessoa, 2017). High levels of negative emotions, such as stress and anxiety, can be seen as extraneous cognitive load because of impact on working memory. High levels of negative emotion are a response to a perceived threat. The learner then allocates some portion of working memory to dealing with this perceived threat. Precious working memory is now not available to attend to other important data and engage in decision-making. In one study, paramedics in an anxiety-provoking situation demonstrated an impaired ability to recall vital information needed to provide care (LeBlanc, 2009).

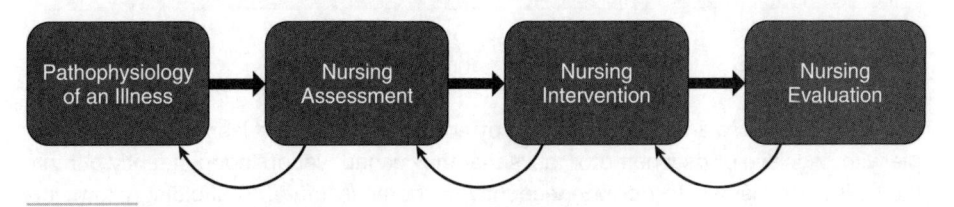

Pathophysiology of an Illness → Nursing Assessment → Nursing Intervention → Nursing Evaluation

FIGURE 3.1 Illustration of designing instruction: chunking.

TABLE 3.1
Designing Instruction: Chunking

Educator Dialogue	Strategy/Purpose
Today, we're going to talk about nursing care of a patient in hypovolemic shock. Some of the material will be familiar from Patho and Med Surg I, and some of it will be new. It's complex material, so please stop me as soon as you have a question. To get started, let's refresh what you learned in Patho about cardiac output and perfusion [*educator-lead review*]	Framing Norming Activating prior knowledge
So, now that we've reviewed cardiac output and perfusion, let's make some links to hypovolemia and shock. We are working with a patient who has just undergone a complex abdominal surgery after a gunshot wound. Blood loss was significant. Consider the cardiac output and perfusion issues that are taking place here. [*Next 20 minutes of class time spent on educator-led new content on hypovolemic shock/intravascular depletion*]	Chunking patho content
OK, we're going to do a few polling questions—multiple choice—we'll discuss the answers after everyone's answered.	Checking in with learners
So, now that we've reviewed the patho of shock, let's think about how patients with hypovolemia will present. We said they would be intravascularly depleted—what will that do to the patient's vital signs? Peripheral perfusion assessment? [*Polling questions on signs and symptoms*]	Chunking assessment content Making connections to previous "patho chunk" Checking in with learners
Let's now think about prioritizing nursing care. Based on what we know about how this patient will present and the pathophysiology underlying those symptoms, what are the care priorities? [*Polling questions*]	Chunking nursing care content Making connections to previous "patho and assessment chunks" Checking in with learners
So, once we've done the nursing interventions and implemented medical treatments, how will we determine if the interventions are helping? Think again about patho—what processes are we trying to reverse? What assessment finding will tell us if this is getting better or worse? [*Polling questions*]	Chunking content related to evaluation of interventions Making connections to previous "patho, assessment, and intervention chunks" Checking in with learners

SCAFFOLDING

Scaffolding refers to any technique used by educators to support learners as they grapple with cognitive or psychomotor tasks that they cannot yet do independently but that they will be expected to do independently in the near future. Scaffolding allows the learner to be more successful than would be possible without it. Scaffolding should be "faded" over time so that, eventually, the learner can be successful independently

TABLE 3.2
Designing Instruction: Schema

Educator Dialogue	Strategy/Purpose
Let's discuss fluid balance and the deep structure that links the relationship between water and sodium. Recall the process of osmosis—semipermeable membranes and the *principle that water follows sodium*.	Activating prior knowledge Reflection on a schema
As you recall this prior knowledge, walk me through your understanding to explain the shift of the sodium and water.	Begin to activate prior learning using the schema as a scaffold to the deep structure of fluid shifts in the body.
Let's take our fluid balance conversation one step further. Think about the principle of water following sodium. Walk me through your thinking of the relationship between sodium and water in hyper/hypoisotonic cells.	Using the schema scaffold to build further on the content knowledge and to compare and contrast cell types

(Taber, 2018). Examples of scaffolding may include providing cues during a simulation to steer the learner in the right direction, modeling behaviors and thought processes, allowing the use of cognitive aids, and posing a reflective question to help the learner focus on relevant information and/or to activate prior knowledge. Previously cited techniques, as referenced earlier, can also be considered scaffolding, including framing, activating prior knowledge, and chunking.

The use of a schema is another example of scaffolding. Weidman and Baker (2015) discuss the use of schemas as a way to help learners understand a concept and then use the knowledge derived from this understanding to make connections to the same concept but in a different context. The schema represents *deep structure* of a concept (Weidman & Baker, 2015). For example, in Table 3.2, the educator has used a schema to both activate prior knowledge and guide the learner's use of the knowledge to build on the deep structure of the relationship between water and sodium to later understand fluid shifts in the body. The use of a schema as a scaffold provides a common foundation for the learner to use and reflect on multiple patient care situations moving forward.

RETRIEVAL PRACTICES: BLOCKED SPACING VS. INTERLEAVING

The use of blocking, or chunking, information is an opportunity for the educator to both control the amount of content presented in a specific period and provide an opportunity for the learner to recall relevant information. Blocking and spacing are forms of retrieval practices—strategies used to help learners recall information to enhance their learning. They are strategies that engage learners to pull out and use the existing knowledge from their content base. As an example, thinking that one knows the name of the first female astronaut, and yet using a strategy of taking the time to struggle and find out (Sally Kirsten Ride, not the first female but the first American female) better cements that memory pathway. It is in the struggle of *not quite remembering* and returning and actively taking part in sense-making that is important to keep in mind. Retrieval practices that include chunking content to manage cognitive load and then spacing the time frame before returning to that content create meaningful approaches for transfer of learning to long-term memory.

When compared with other more common strategies, which include rereading a textbook passage and reviewing lecture notes or study guides, a learner's overall performance is far more enhanced when educators use intentional strategies that guide learners to *recall* content *in the moment* (Weidman & Baker, 2015). In their work, Weidman and Baker (2015) support the theory that spaced repeated retrieval is more effective than simply restudying content. What this means for us as nurse educators is that teaching something once may not be effective. Creatively identifying ways to guide students to retrieve that content will move them to successfully achieve the outcomes. Spacing out content blocks by stretching the interval of time between periods creates deeper learning as the learner goes back to retrieve content to use again (Agarwal, 2019; Firth et al., 2019).

Retrieval practice strategies provide an opportunity for a dynamic critical conversation. Challenging learners to retrieve knowledge *in the moment* is oftentimes a struggle for our learners. As contemporary educators, intentional use of retrieval practices can be a powerful and meaningful strategy to role model content. We have already discussed blocking, chunking, and spaced retrieval practices. Interleaving is a type of retrieval spaced blocking and a practice that nurse educators can role model because professional nurses do this intuitively in everyday practice when they go back and forth between medication administration, nursing assessment and so on.

The strategies of interleaving and blocked spacing are similar but inherently different (Agarwal, 2019). Blocked spacing is an approach in which learners revise their content knowledge over a spaced-out period of time. Interleaving is switching between ideas within a set period. Here again, the educator's use of time is an important factor. A topic is introduced; the educator leaves the topic and then switches to another topic *within the same period of time*. The difference between blocked spacing and interleaving is the variance of *over time* versus *within a period of time*. Figure 3.2 illustrates this concept. Using Figure 3.2 to outline an example in nursing, Topic 1 might be *hypertonic* fluid balance pathophysiology, nursing assessment, and intervention, whereas Topic 2 might be *hypotonic* fluid balance pathophysiology, nursing assessment, and intervention.

While both strategies are similar, their benefits are different. They both boost memory because the spacing effect is spread out; thus, the learner has an opportunity to recall with some forgetting accounted for. The added benefit of interleaving is that it enhances learners' inductive reasoning capacity because they are engaged in moving from one topic to the next without complete understanding of the first topic. This strategy is not to suggest that educators interleave completely different topics (i.e., switching between fluid balance and infection). The key to successful interleaving is that the *topics are similar* and *mixed together* to encourage the learner to apply learned content in a different way as they switch between topics. Learners use pieces of content from each topic to inform their understanding as they move between the topics to piece together the whole (Agarwal, 2019; Firth et al., 2019).

In an effort to support the effectiveness of interleaving, a study in 2008 by Kornell and Bjork examined this strategy with art students. Instead of presenting artwork by one

	Week 1	Week 2
Blocked (A)	Topic 1	Topic 2
	Topic 1	Topic 2
	Topic 1	Topic 2
	Topic 1	Topic 2
	Topic 1	Topic 2
	Topic 1	Topic 2
Interleaved (B)	Topic 2	Topic 1
	Topic 2	Topic 1
	Topic 2	Topic 1
	Topic 1	Topic 2
	Topic 1	Topic 2
	Topic 1	Topic 2

FIGURE 3.2 Illustration of designing instruction: interleaving.

artist in a blocked fashion, artwork across different artists was presented using interleaving. Students who were engaged with interleaving strategies had higher test scores on identifying artists' work than students using blocked spacing strategies. Interleaving provided intentional and consecutive opportunities for comparing and contrasting across artists in a period of time versus consecutive artists over a period of time. When educators use an interleaved approach to teaching, they are helping learners to see similarities, connections, and differences within a context that ultimately develops a deeper understanding and meaning for the learner and a better chance of transferring that learning into long-term memory. Interleaving makes the learning event more challenging and, in the end, more effective, as this style of learning is consistent with actual everyday nursing practice. Think about the nurse's first encounter with a patient. The patient is not likely to present to the nurse with an index card outlining everything to which the nurse should be paying attention. Nurses may have a solid understanding of the pathophysiology of their patients who present with dehydration before they enter the room. Yet the nurse must discern what assessments need to be made in that moment based on the nature of the questions that the nurse will ask; the objective findings (e.g., lab results on electrolytes, urine output); and the subjective findings, (e.g., reports of being weak and tired). All inform the nature and appropriateness of interventions moving forward.

Let's examine how interleaving can be incorporated into the earlier discussion in which the educator was using a schema as a scaffold to build the learners' understanding of fluid balance shifts and the subsequent nursing assessments and interventions that follow (Table 3.3).

The teaching strategies described in this chapter are all aimed at helping learners not just learn content but also learn how to apply that content to solve real nursing problems. These strategies all place the learners at the center of the experience as the educator seeks to understand their unique thought processes. Learners may well find some of these techniques quite challenging; in fact, educators will be challenged as they learn to skillfully use these strategies. The long-term payoff of these "desirable difficulties" is learning that "sticks" and can be retrieved for repeated application to novel problems.

TABLE 3.3

Designing Instruction: Interleaving

Educator Dialogue	Strategy/Purpose
(Note: Dialogue below picks up from Table 3.2.) Let's take our fluid balance conversation one step further. Think about the principle of water following sodium. Walk me through your thinking of the relationship between sodium and water in hyper/hypoisotonic cells	Using the schema scaffold to build further on the content knowledge and to compare and contrast cell types
Now that you have reviewed your prior knowledge on hyper/hypoisotonic cells, let's discuss the nature of the shift that is happening in and outside of the cells to explain our hypotonic cellular environment and the electrolyte concentrations. Let's do a few polling questions. Let's discuss the nature of the shift that is happening in and outside of the cells to explain our hypertonic cellular environment and the electrolyte concentrations. Let's do a few polling questions.	Chunk of 10 minutes on hypotonic fluid balance Checking in Interleave to move to hypertonic cellular environment—10-minute chunk Checking in
With a hypotonic cellular environment, walk me through your thinking of what you might see physically. Let's do some polling questions on nursing assessment. Differentiate that from hypertonic cellular environments. Walk me through your thinking of what you might see physically. Let's do some polling questions on nursing assessment.	Interleave to hypotonic fluid environments and 10-minute chunk on nursing assessment components. Checking in Interleave to hypertonic fluid environments and 10-minute chunk on nursing assessment components. Checking in
I have a clinical exemplar that I would like to get your thinking on. Millie Larson is a 78-year-old female who presents to the ED confused and lethargic. Her daughter Dina has informed you that she doesn't think Millie has been taking her medication and doesn't think she's been eating or drinking anything over the last couple of days. Understanding the nature of fluid balance informs our nursing assessments. Walk me through your thinking on Millie's physiologic clinical presentation of fluid balance. How does her presentation inform your nursing assessment and the necessary assessment components?	Interleave to nursing assessments of each cellular condition without specific label whereby learners inductively apply their learning.
Let's discuss Millie's fluid imbalance, the nature of the fluid shift that is happening, and your assessment findings and move to appropriate nursing interventions.	Interleave to 10-minute chunk on nursing interventions for fluid balance deficits.

References

Agarwal, P. K. (2019). Retrieval practice & Bloom's taxonomy: Do students need fact knowledge before higher order learning? *Journal of Educational Psychology, 111*(2), 189–209. https://doi.org/10.1037/edu0000282

Argyris, C. (1992). *Reasoning, learning and action: Individual and organizational.* Jossey-Bass.

Argyris, C., & Schon, D. (1974). *Theory in practice.* Jossey-Bass.

Chase, W. G., & Simon, H. A. (1973). The mind's eye in chess. In W. G. Chase (Ed.), *Visual information processing* (pp. 215–281). Academic Press.

Firth, J., Rivers, I., & Boyle, J. (2019) A systematic review of interleaving as a concept learning strategy: A study protocol. *Social Science Protocols, 2*, 1–7. https://doi.org/10.7565/ssp.2019.2650

Forneris, S. G. (2004). Exploring the attributes of critical thinking: A conceptual basis. *International Journal of nursing education scholarship, 1*(1). https://doi.org/10.2202/1548-923X.1026

Forneris, S. G., & Fey, M. (Eds.). (2018). *Critical conversations: The NLN guide for teaching thinking.* Wolters Kluwer.

Gobet, F. (2005). Chunking models of expertise: Implications for education. *Applied Cognitive Psychology, 19*(2), 183–204. https://doi.org/10.1002/acp.1110

Josephsen, J. (2015). Cognitive load theory and nursing simulation: An integrative review. *Clinical Simulation in Nursing, 11*(5), 259–267. https://doi.org/10.1016/j.ecns.2015.02.004

Kornell, N., & Bjork, R. A. (2008). Learning concepts and categories: Is spacing the "enemy of induction"? *Psychological Science, 19*, 585–592. https://doi.org/10.1111/j.1467-9280.2008.02127.x

LeBlanc, V. R. (2009). The effects of acute stress on performance: Implications for health professions education. *Academic Medicine, 84*(10), S25–S33. https://doi.org/10.1097/ACM.0b013e3181b37b8f

LeBlanc, V. R., McConnell, M. M., & Monteiro, S. D. (2015). Predictable chaos: A review of the effects of emotions on attention, memory and decision making. *Advances in Health Sciences Education, 20*(1), 265–282. https://doi.org/10.1007/s10459-014-9516-6

Meguerdichian, M., Walker, K., & Bajaj, K. (2016). Working memory is limited: Improving knowledge transfer by optimizing simulation through cognitive load theory. *BMJ Simulation & Technology Enhanced Learning, 2*(4), 131–138. http://dx.doi.org/10.1136/bmjstel-2015-000098

Mezirow, J. (1978). Perspective transformation. *Adult Education, 28*(2), 100–110. https://doi.org/10.1177/074171367802800202

Mezirow, J. (1990). *Fostering critical reflection in adulthood: A guide to transformative and emancipatory learning.* Jossey-Bass.

Mezirow, J. (2000). *Learning as transformation: Critical perspectives on a theory in progress.* Jossey-Bass.

Pessoa, L. (2017). A network model of the emotional brain. *Trends in Cognitive Sciences, 21*(5), 357–371. https://doi.org/10.1016/j.tics.2017.03.002

Ruiter, D. J., van Kesteren, M. T., & Fernandez, G. (2012). How to achieve synergy between medical education and cognitive neuroscience? An exercise on prior knowledge in understanding. *Advances in Health Sciences Education, 17*(2), 225–240. https://doi.org/10.1007/s10459-010-9244-5

Schon, D. (1983). *The reflective practitioner.* Basic Books.

Schon, D. (1987). *Educating the reflective practitioner.* Jossey Bass.

Sweller, J. (1994). Cognitive load theory, learning difficulty, and instructional design. *Learning and Instruction, 4*(4), 295–312. https://doi.org/10.1016/0959-4752(94)90003-5

Taber, K. (2018). Scaffolding learning: Principles for effective teaching and the design of classroom resources. In M. Abend (Ed.), *Effective teaching and learning: Perspectives,* strategies and implementation (pp. 1–43). Nova Science.

Van Merriënboer, J. J., & Sweller, J. (2010). Cognitive load theory in health professional education: Design principles and strategies. *Medical Educator*, *44*(1), 85–93. https://doi.org/10.1111/j.1365-2923.2009.03498.x

Weidman, J., & Baker, K. (2015). The cognitive science of learning: Concepts and strategies for the educator and learner. *Neuroscience in Anesthesiology and Perioperative Medicine*, *121*(6), 1586–1599. https://doi.org/10.1213/ANE.0000000000000890

4

Course

The final step of any learning encounter is ensuring that the learning will be carried forward. Course is the final phase of the critical conversation. Course is defined as setting future correct action. The learning that occurred from the conversation during Content is applied to future decisions, both short and long term. The educator's ability to move fluidly between Content and Course makes up the dynamic and critical nature of this conversation. In this final chapter, we will introduce specific strategies that educators can use with learners that build on and engage learner Content knowledge while also transferring that knowledge (Course) for use in different contexts.

During Content, we discussed how the educator uses a variety of learning strategies to help learners connect concepts and information within a domain of learning. These connections form mental models, or schemas, which are stored in long-term memory. These schemas are repeatedly retrieved by learners as they solve novel problems, or as they compare and contrast what is known to what is not yet known. The educator focus is to not only deliver Content, but to also take time to discern how the learner interprets and understands that Content. The use of time is dynamic, taking time to mentor learners with strategies that cement knowledge pathways. Similarly, the concept of time is central to Course; taking time for the desirable difficulties that result in deep learning and the dynamic learning conversation using strategies that build on familiar cognitive schemas to set future correct action (Forneris & Fey, 2018; Weidman & Baker, 2015).

TEACHING AND LEARNING STRATEGIES FOR COURSE
Metacognition

Simply stated, metacognition is thinking about your thinking (Weidman & Baker, 2015). During Course, the educator guides learners to think about their thinking as it relates to an action taken. This can specifically be an action taken in an event or perhaps action in the form of a response to a question. The strategy of strengthening learner metacognition involves learners reflecting in and on action (Schon, 1983, 1987). The nature of this reflection engages a critical dialogue whereby the educator is curious not about the action or the response provided but more around what knowledge or thinking led to the actions or response provided by the learner. The educator creates this critical dialogue to direct learners to reflect *on the action* (i.e., action taken, or response provided) to get in touch with their *knowing in action* (i.e., tacit or intuitive knowledge or thinking) that guided the action. For instance, read the following excerpt:

> Sheila, an experienced RN, returns to assess her patient after having started intravenous fluids. The patient appears short of breath and verbalizes having more difficulty catching a breath. After listening to the patient's lungs, getting an O_2 sat and respiratory rate, she shuts off the IV and raises the head of the bed. These actions all take less than 1 minute.

Using a critical reflection dialogue technique to practice a metacognitive activity (i.e., thinking about your thinking), the educator might say the dialogue found in Table 4.1.

If Sheila were to describe that her thinking was really guided in the moment by her knowing (1) the patient's medical diagnosis of dehydration and chronic congestive heart failure (CHF); (2) the implications of hearing crackles that were not present upon the initial assessment earlier; and (3) the pathophysiology of fluid balance issues with CHF; she would be providing a clear example of the *knowing-in-action* (tacit knowing or, in a sense, intuitive knowing) informing her actions. They were tacit *in the moment* when she was quickly and accurately working with the patient, yet all this knowledge was guiding

TABLE 4.1

Example of Critical Reflection Dialogue Technique

Educator Dialogue	Strategy/Purpose
Sheila, let's discuss this patient encounter to get a better understanding of your thinking or knowledge that led to your actions.	Framing to set the context
I see that when you walked into the patient's room, you quickly assessed the patient by listening to the lung sounds, checked O_2 sats, respiratory rate; and then shut off the IV and raised the head of the bed…all things that were spot on with the assessment and initial intervention.	Use objective data Share your perspective
Could you walk me through your thinking around the steps you were taking?	Reflection on action to get at the in-action knowing that led to the actions she took

her regardless of whether it was evident to her in the moment. Only when she reflects on it will it come to the surface. As Schon (1983, 1987) would suggest, it is only when we guide learners to intentionally reflect on their actions and *the thinking guiding the action* will all aspects of their knowing be revealed (i.e., tacit knowing). This is a skill that experienced nurses use and practice. As experienced nurses, we are always thinking about our actions and what drove us to those actions. We are building and reinforcing our knowing and, therefore, our tacit knowing and those knowledge pathways that deepen our expertise. This tacit knowing is at work for us the next time we encounter a similar experience.

We previously mentioned that engaging our learners successfully requires the educator to move back and forth within a dialogue between Content and Course. This is best illustrated when the educator moves from forming a schema (Content). to application of the schema in a similar context (Content), to application in a different context (Course). The nature of the metacognitive dialogue and the time taken to understand learner perspective is an invaluable skill by an educator to help set Course. In doing so, metacognitive skills are strengthened early on. Learners can provide their own insights and perspectives. They can also confirm correct and incorrect thinking and rationale reinforcing the knowledge pathways and more easily apply correct thinking to a future context.

Collaborative Cognition

Understanding cognition is becoming increasingly more complex. While cognition was once simply understood as the mind's ability to process information, cognitive science continues to evolve. Earlier in this monograph, you read about situated cognition such that the mind processes information as a dynamic process between a subject and its environment, not just one's mind (Roth & Jornet, 2013). Collaborative cognition derives from collaborative learning whereby two or more learners are coming together to work toward achieving a learning outcome. The key to effective learning in this sense is that each learner will gain new knowledge from the collaboration (Kirschner et al., 2018). Kirschner et al. (2018) go on to further explain that when collaborative learning takes place successfully, it introduces a collective working memory. Recall from Chapter 3, Content, the discussion on working memory as the ability to process information, to *keep multiple balls in the air*. Working memory is also sensitive to extraneous cognitive load. With collaborative cognition, multiple working memories are brought together in a dialogue with a richer exchange of information and new processing. The collaboration becomes, in a sense, a scaffold for the learners—making use of more than one brain and working memory to reach new and different conclusions. While collaborative cognition can reduce the demands and loads of working memory in some ways, it is still sensitive to extraneous cognitive load. Take, for example, group work that requires all members of the group to have the same level of information. If one learner has little knowledge while another learner has more knowledge, the imbalance can introduce extraneous cognitive load and the collaboration may not be successful (Kirschner et al., 2018).

In nursing education, a concrete example of collaborative cognition can be illustrated with peer mentoring. Literature in nursing education research supports the effectiveness of peer mentoring using the same collaborative cognition framework described earlier (i.e., multiple perspectives, richer exchange of information and processing, sense of support, gaining of self-confidence) (Benner, 1984; Giddens et al., 2010; Giordana & Wedin, 2010; Ross, 2019). Outcomes gained through collaborative thinking and learning together supported the equal exchange of being both mentor and mentee. Communication changed with a deeper appreciation of others' viewpoints and rationale that enhanced commitment to achieving learning outcomes. Key to these successful peer mentoring experiences, however, was the balance of foundational knowledge going into the collaborative work such that intrinsic cognitive load was enhanced (i.e., the goal of the learning itself) while extraneous cognitive load was reduced (i.e., equal foundational knowledge) (Table 4.2).

Analogical Transfer

Engaging learners to use the Content that they just acquired in a new and different way and apply it to a future Context requires intentional teaching strategies. Analogical transfer is one option that creates a rich dialogue with learners, as the educator can pose a future dilemma that challenges them to use recently acquired Content knowledge and walk through a future Context. Weidman and Baker (2015) define *analogical transfer* as using content or a solution that a learner has successfully experienced or understands and transferring that same solution to a similar problem in a different context or situation. Content serves as the first opportunity for the development of their mental model or schema for understanding. In Course, the key to successful analogical transfer is using the schema that the educator helped the learner to build. Creating and using a schema that establishes or cements a solid foundational understanding of the principle being taught to achieve a learning outcome is the most successful for learning retention. The learner's ability to use the schema to discern the same deep structure in a different context is at the heart of learning. When a learner encounters a new problem that on the surface is different than the previous problem, yet the problems share the same relevant deep structure, the ability to transfer that learning is much greater (Weidman & Baker, 2015). It is the use of the schema representing the deep understanding that will help learners to begin using their content knowledge for problem solving. An example is comparing nursing interventions for a patient with hypovolemic shock versus a patient with septic shock; the learner must have a solid understanding of the deep structure of the mechanisms of cardiac output (i.e., preload, afterload, and cardiac contractility). The similarity between these two conditions is low cardiac output due to intravascular volume depletion. Components of cardiac output comprise the schema. If learners use components of cardiac output to explain intravascular volume depletion, they will more likely successfully transfer this explanation to further explain the rationale behind why the treatment approaches differ (i.e., septic shock needs vasopressors and volume while hypovolemic shock needs volume).

Another example of how analogical transfer can be applied directly in nursing education is best illustrated in the work of Dreifuerst (2009, 2010) through *reflection beyond action*. This form of reflection occurs at the end of a dialogue and encourages learners to participate in a reflective learning activity whereby they look back at a past learning experience while they simultaneously anticipate forward. Dreifuerst (2009) suggests that anticipating forward can be analogous to an expert nurse using intuition or intuitive

TABLE 4.2
Designing Instruction: Collaborative Cognition

Educator Dialogue	Strategy/Purpose
Our conversations in class have focused on fluid balance—both understanding the implications for our nursing assessments, interventions, and evaluation of our care. As we have discussed previously, understanding the nature of fluid balance informs our nursing assessments and best care interventions moving forward.	Framing and reflecting on knowledge acquired
We have talked about Millie and Adam. Both cover opposite ends of the continuum of age, and this informs how we might think about fluid balance shifts.	Framing and reflecting on schema supporting our knowledge
An important conversation as we think about using our knowledge going forward might be to reflect on nursing education to prevent future fluid-balance deviations like Millie's (i.e., aging adult not eating or drinking) and Adam's (i.e., young athlete losing fluid on a soccer field) from repeating. How might we create patient education materials as tools to support community nursing efforts for Millie's family caregivers and Jonah's coaching staff at the school?	Framing the learning in a new context
We are going to work in small groups. The purpose of this group activity is to combine your thinking and knowledge on fluid balance and design the following for use by senior clients and adolescent clients and their support systems to prevent extreme fluid balance situations. Specifically, address the following: 1. Guidelines for at-risk clients to prevent imbalances 2. Assessment strategies to detect signs and symptoms of fluid imbalance 3. Interventions when imbalances are detected 4. Resources for families and support systems to understand the need for assessment strategies, necessary interventions, and the guidelines for prevention	Reflection on moving knowledge forward in a new context

thinking as described by Benner's seminal work From Novice to Expert (1984). In this way, the instructor poses a future encounter engaging the learner in a critical conversation and posing a "what if" scenario. The learner uses recent past learning experience and anticipates what may change or remain the same. The educator role models *anticipatory reflection* by encouraging the learner to think beyond the boundaries of a current situation. Using analogical transfer as a mechanism for anticipatory reflection requires the learner to actively and critically reflect on the schema that the educator helped to build. By doing so, the learner cements foundational knowledge and can now apply and explain knowledge in both current and future contexts. Through anticipation of what might change, the learner generates new meaning that may inform a future encounter (Dreifuerst, 2010). Let us pick up the conversation started in Content and the example of

TABLE 4.3

Designing Instruction: Analogical Transfer

Educator Dialogue	Strategy/Purpose
(Note: Dialogue below picks up from Chapter 3, Table 3.3, p. 22) I have a clinical exemplar that I would like to get your thinking on.	
Millie Larson is a 78-year-old female who presents to the ED confused and lethargic. Her daughter Dina has informed you that she doesn't think Millie has been taking her medication and doesn't hink she's been eating or drinking anything over the last couple of days.	
Understanding the nature of fluid balance informs our nursing assessments. Walk me through your thinking on Millie's physiologic clinical presentation of fluid balance. How does her presentation inform your nursing assessment and the necessary assessment components?	Interleave to nursing assessment of fluid balance condition without specific label of hypo/iso/hypertonic whereby learners inductively apply their learning.
Let's discuss Millie's fluid imbalance and the nature of the fluid shift that is happening plus your assessment findings and move to appropriate nursing interventions.	Interleave to 20-minute chunk on nursing interventions for fluid-balance deficits.
The focus of our conversation has been on understanding nursing assessments and interventions when working with patients experiencing disruptions with fluid balance. Understanding the nature of fluid balance informs our nursing assessments and best care interventions moving forward.	Activating prior knowledge using schema
Millie Larson is an elderly female client who has not been drinking fluids. She is a clinical presentation of dehydration [fluid balance/shifts]. Let's think beyond Millie and discuss our thinking using a clinical exemplar of a young male adolescent athlete, Adam, who is at soccer camp and on the field for 8 hours in 85°F temp with a dewpoint of 70°F. He is sweating profusely, yet he is drinking water while on the field. He presents to the ED with a clinical picture of dehydration also.	Framing the analogy
Differentiate Adam's physiologic clinical presentation from that of Millie's. Describe how the presentations are the same and where they are different, and why. Discuss the interventions for Adam that a nurse might anticipate and why.	Analogical transfer Note: The surface structure of these clinical presentations is different (i.e., isotonic dehydration vs. hypotonic dehydration). The deep structure and schema (i.e., fluid balance and water follows sodium) stay consistent. Understanding the deep structure helps learners apply the knowledge to a different patient care context (i.e., Adam's clinical presentation) to discuss nursing assessment and intervention.

interleaving. The educator was guiding learners in a conversation on fluid balance and was presenting a clinical exemplar of an aging adult, Millie, experiencing dehydration and fluid imbalance (Table 4.3).

The teaching strategies described in this chapter are all aimed at helping learners build on familiar cognitive schemas to set future correct action. Course is a dynamic learning conversation that further cements learning pathways to long-term memory storage and retrieval. Here again, the learner continues to be at the center of experience. The educator is actively curious about how learners see content, think about the Content and use the Content within a Context and again beyond the immediate Context. As was discussed throughout this monograph, these learning strategies do not come without a bit of work on the part of the learner and educator. The outcomes outweigh the struggle, as the conversations that evolve and the deep learning that takes place set the course for future lifelong learning. As contemporary nurse educators, our goal is to prepare future professional nurses who can achieve excellence in their own practice of nursing. This takes time and intention. As Aristotle said so eloquently, "*Excellence is never an accident. It is always the result of high intention, sincere effort, and intelligent execution; it represents the wise choice of many alternatives—choice, not chance, determines your destiny*" (Seale, 2020).

References

Benner, P. (1984). *From novice to expert*. Addison-Wesley.

Dreifuerst, K. T. (2009). The essentials of debriefing in simulation learning: A concept analysis. *Nursing Education Perspectives, 30*(2), 109–114.

Dreifuerst, K. T. (2010). *Debriefing for meaningful learning: Fostering development of clinical reasoning through simulation* [Unpublished doctoral dissertation]. Indiana University.

Forneris, S. G., & Fey, M. (Eds.) (2018). *Critical conversations: The NLN guide for teaching thinking*. National League for Nursing.

Giddens, S. S., Helton, C., & Hope, K. L. (2010). Student peer mentoring in a community-based nursing clinical experience. *Nursing Education Perspectives, 31*(1), 23–27.

Giordana, S., & Wedin, B. (2010). Peer mentoring for multiple levels of nursing students. *Nursing Education Perspective, 31*(6), 304–396.

Kirschner, P. A., Sweller, J., Kirschner, F., & Zambrano, J. R. (2018). From cognitive load theory to collaborative cognitive load theory. *International Journal of Computer Supported Collaborative Learning, 13*, 213–233. https://doi.org/10.1007/s11412-018-9277-y

Ross, J. G. (2019). Repetitive practice with peer mentoring to foster skill competence and retention in baccalaureate nursing students. *Nursing Education Perspectives, 40*(1), 48–49. https://10.1097/01.NEP.0000000000000358

Roth, W.-M., & Jornet, A. (2013). Situated cognition. *WIREs Cognitive Science, 4*, 463–478. https://doi.org/10.1002/wcs.1242

Schon, D. (1983). *The reflective practitioner*. Basic Books, Inc.

Schon, D. (1987). *Educating the reflective practitioner*. Jossey Bass, Inc.

Seale, Q. (2020). *113 Aristotle quotes that changed western history forever*. Retrieved from https://www.keepinspiring.me/aristotle-quotes/

Weidman, J., & Baker, K. (2015). The cognitive science of learning: Concepts and strategies for the educator and learner. *Neuroscience in Anesthesiology and Perioperative Medicine, 121*(6), 1586–1599. https://doi.org/10.1213/ANE.0000000000000890

Epilogue

With the first and now this second volume in the National League for Nursing's *Critical Conversations* series, nurse educators have in their hands a powerful set of tools to guide them in the transformation needed in nursing education. In both volumes, the authors provide examples and specific directions that nurse educators can use to engage learners in active thinking in action as they consider best approaches within clinical situations. This guidance is grounded in knowledge from learning science and models of experiential, situated, and constructivist learning. It is also informed by the well-known Dreyfus Novice to Expert model of skills acquisition (Benner, 1984; Dreyfus, 1992, 2001; Dreyfus et al., 1988; Hooper-Kyriakidis et al., 2011). This model of human intelligence tells us that skills acquisition in a practice can be achieved only through practical experience that integrates disengaged, abstracted knowledge—knowing *that*—and engaged practical knowledge—knowing *how* (Hooper-Kyriakidis et al., 2011). When theoretical and practical knowledge and learning are integrated, nurses are better able to build the skills they need to draw on abstract knowledge as they respond within unique, evolving clinical situations (Benner et al., 2010). Beginning in the first volume and continuing in this second volume of *Critical Conversations*, the authors have offered nurse educators the structure and means by which to do this important work of integration.

In this second volume, the authors take us deeper into the structure of the 3 Cs—Context, Content, and Course—and, through specific examples, advise nurse educators on how to set up classes and learning experiences based on this structure. Most importantly, the authors use this structure to center learning in the teacher-learner relationship and in the use of clinically focused, authentic dialogue. When the teacher focuses classroom learning on the client, patient family, or community and their unique needs—and asks, in essence, "What do we care about here?"—learners are offered the opportunity to try out and shape their thinking while receiving support and coaching from the teacher and other learners. Learners also have the benefit of engaging in dialogue and conversation with the teacher—an experienced nurse—as they think through a complex clinical question together. The value of this collegial role-modeling as the experienced nurse portrays the practice for the learners cannot be overstated. Through these authentic problem-solving experiences, nurse learners practice the real skills they need in clinical reasoning—for example, questioning, observing, and attending to the salient features of a situation. In this way, the examples and guidelines offered in this monograph have put forward a plan for extending experiential learning into the classroom while integrating theoretical knowledge. In addition, the authors have made an important contribution to closing the gap between theoretical knowing *that* and practical, experiential knowing *how*, a necessary step to positively transform nursing education and better prepare new nurses for practice.

Lisa Day, PhD, RN, CNE, FAAN, ANEF
Professor, Clinician Educator
University of New Mexico College of Nursing

References

Benner, P., Sutphen, M., Leonard, V., & Day, L. (2010). *Educating nurses: A call for radical transformation*. Jossey-Bass.

Benner, P. E. (1984). *From novice to expert: Excellence and power in clinical nursing practice*. Addison-Wesley.

Dreyfus, H. L. (1992). *What computers still can't do: A critique of artificial reason*. MIT Press.

Dreyfus, H. L. (2001). *On the Internet*. Routledge.

Dreyfus, S. E., Athanasiou, T., & Dreyfus, H. L. (1988). *Mind over machine: The power of human intuition and expertise in the era of the computer*. Free Press.

Hooper-Kyriakidis, P. L., Stannard, D., & Benner, P. E. (2011). *Clinical wisdom and interventions in acute and critical care: A thinking-in-action approach* (2nd ed.). Springer.